By
Choice

By Choice

A Novel by

PatriciaAnn A. Grant

authorHOUSE®

AuthorHouse™
1663 Liberty Drive
Bloomington, IN 47403
www.authorhouse.com
Phone: 1 (800) 839-8640

Published by AuthorHouse 04/14/2015

ISBN: 978-1-5049-0683-8 (sc)
ISBN: 978-1-5049-0682-1 (e)

Library of Congress Control Number: 2015905972

Print information available on the last page.

Any people depicted in stock imagery provided by Thinkstock are models,
and such images are being used for illustrative purposes only.
Certain stock imagery © Thinkstock.

This book is printed on acid-free paper.

Because of the dynamic nature of the Internet, any web addresses or links contained in
this book may have changed since publication and may no longer be valid. The views
expressed in this work are solely those of the author and do not necessarily reflect the
views of the publisher, and the publisher hereby disclaims any responsibility for them.

In Dedication

This is not a book about "my" life before meeting my husband. Any reference to it is merely given for relevance, comparison and reflection. This is a book about compassion, love, and choice. This is a book about Devine Faith in our Heavenly Father and His Love for each of us.

This is a story inspired from our lives but told in a fiction-based novel.

This book is written to give *hope to the hopeless* and *faith to the faithless*.
It is inspired by a need for such a book;
the tremendous love, compassion and devotion
of my husband's parents and siblings,
the dedicated support from my own parents and wonderful sons,
the caring and gently spirit of my wonderful and loving Husband, and
my desire to write *"our" story* divulging *"our" choices*.

Contents

Preface

Reflections and Expectations

As a child, a teenager, and probably most of my young adult life, I assumed every day would be much like the day before with minor variations. Sameness each day in that I would arise, clean up – showering, brushing my teeth, fixing my hair, putting on my makeup, making breakfast and tending to the regular expected chores of the day, such a school or work, etc. Doesn't everyone? Aren't we supposed to?

The old story that my Grandma used to say, "God doesn't want you to know about tomorrow – that's His plan" never has been so real before as it has been over the last eighteen years. Good thing for all of us that the Master's plan excludes knowing our future.

Today I still get up each morning and do those things for which I am expected to. After raising three sons, those chores changed a bit over the years but not all that much. My household is probably much like yours.

As I think about writing my thoughts, I want you to enjoy reading this book and know there is a wonderful true-to-life fairy tale about to unravel before your eyes. Not many folks are privileged to live out a fairy tale or perhaps most folks would not title their lives that way. Well, I am going to do that to mine, to my Husband's and mine because God has blessed us. Keep reading it gets better.

Remember no matter how wonderful I paint my life, I too have my down days and down times. Although I view my life as wonderful today, it certainly has seen a number of terrible times, too many to remember or care to write about. That's what makes this new life, the life I chose when I married a Traumatic Brain Injury ("TBI") survivor, a "storybook fantasy" in the flesh! Yours can be too, if you want it and are willing and able to let God play an active part in your life.

As I recall the record of my Husband's life, this is hearsay testimony but verified to the best of his knowledge and memory, and that of his family.

Who's Who Within "By Choice"

Peter Gallagher	The Brain Injured 16-yr. Old
Dan & Ellie Gallaghers	Pete's Parents
Jane Gallagher	Pete's Sister
Stanley Gallagher	Pete's Brother
Billy Gallagher	Pete's Brother
Lori Jenkins	Pete's First Girlfriend
Shirley Christianson	Peter's First Fiancée
Steffan Lewinski	First Roommate
Blake Cavenelli	Second Roommate
Nanette Peters, Sullivan, Squires, Grant	The Love of Peter's Life
Jimmy Peters	Nanette's Brother
Jake Daniel Sullivan Squires	Nanette's First Son
Jamie Paul Sullivan Squires	Nanette's Second Son
Theodore Jason Squires	Nanette's Third Son
Connie Daley	Teddy's Wife/Nanette's Daughter-in-Law
Candice Satelli	Jamie's Wife/Nanette's Daughter-in-Law
Ann & Lee Peters	Nanette's Parents
Aunt Gracie Orlin Renaldi	Nanette's Special Aunt
Sam Sullivan	Nanette's First Husband
Erica Sullivan Schmidt	Sam Sullivan's Sister
Bartlett Squires	Nanette's Second Husband
Atty Cory Petrelli	Nanette's First Attorney Employer
Dr. Kirkland	Brain Surgeon
Dr. Theodore Harkins	Peter's Psychiatrist
Dr. Robert Cutler	Psychologist for Couple Therapy
Julie Laughlin	Director of Adult Independent Living Assoc. (AILA)
Judy Collins	DMR – Social Worker
Sally Rigley	Peter's TBI Research Doctor
Pastor Bart Ellington	Peter's Pastor
Pastor Jason Schneider	Pastor of Community Church
Penny Peters	One of Nanette's Best Friends & Sister-in-Law
Penny Murphy	One of Nanette's Best Friends
Lily Reynolds	One of Nanette's Best Friends

Chapter I

Teenage Assumption

It was September 1969 and the world seemed to be so special with tons of promises for Pete Gallagher and his family. Ellie and Dan Gallagher had met in college and married during Dan's senior year. They had lived the normal American life, or so they thought. Dan had served his country in the United States Air Force. They were blessed with three children when Dan was summoned to help build a substantial insurance company in Hawaii. Dan and Ellie had enjoyed their lives and had friends from Seattle, Washington, and Hawaii before moving to Connecticut to continue his work with the insurance company. Since Dan had grown up most of his life on the west coast and Ellie on the east coast, they had plenty of opportunities to travel to visit family and friends. They had built a new home and that brought the birth of their fourth child. Moving to their second house, in West Hartford the family enjoyed various activities that Dan's job afforded them. They were important members of society and their lives were blessed with the activities afforded them. They were living the American dream.

It was a bright and sunny morning and the world lie ahead. Today was the day that Kingswood (now Kingswood-Oxford) a prep school in West Hartford, Connecticut would beat the pants off of Williston Academy in Williston, Massachusetts in their pre-season scrimmage football game. All the right things were in place, but Pete needed to remember to visit the sports shop in town before the bus left. His helmet was a bit small. There should be a guard to be placed up under the back of his helmet in order to protect his neck where his helmet ended and the top of his shoulders began in order to prevent injuries. So a brief excursion to the local sports shop and sixteen year old Pete Gallagher would be ready for the big game.

Pete Gallagher was the first-born son of Ellie and Dan Gallagher. Pete had an older sister, Jane and two younger brothers, Stan and Billy. Today Stan was playing in his own football game where Dan and Ellie were present to watch his game along with Billy. At 18 years old, Jane was very independent and had plans of her own.

Pete visited the local sports shop where he confronted the owner in frustration, as his time was so limited.

"What do you mean you don't have any neck guards? But I need one for my game today," said Pete. "My time is very limited."

"Sorry Pete. I'm out of stock just now. Why don't you come back some time the middle of next week. I'm sure they'll be in by then."

"But the game is today."

"Sorry, Pete."

Pete thought for a moment. He didn't have time to go somewhere else. The bus would be leaving soon and he needed to be on it. He knew he should have looked into getting this guard a long time ago.

Pete Gallagher was already 6 feet 3 inches tall and still growing. His parents had a hard time keeping up with Pete's continuing changes in size. Either he grew taller or his bodybuilding made Pete have a very dense and muscular body. He intense course of exercises made Peter develop quickly and thus keeping up with his changing sizes were a challenge. Since he continued to lift weights, his body would continue to go through physical changes and size would continue to be an issue – a good issue, but nonetheless an issue probably more for his parents than for Pete. After all, what does it matter to a 16-year-old junior in high school if he has to have new clothes every month – an irrelevant concern at 16 years old? Pete

Gallagher was more in tune to what his body strength would mean to be fit to play a great football game – nothing else mattered except maybe Lori.

Pete hurried up the hill and down the street just in time as his teammates were loading the bus with massive amounts of gear. All gear was checked and all were accounted for. The bus fired up its engine in no time and they were off. The highway was busy, but the driver was skillful and knew just how to get through the traffic. They couldn't be late. The team had looked forward to this game for a long time.

"Hey, Pete," said Mike. "We thought you had forgotten about the game. You're running a bit late, buddy."

"Yeah, I know," replied Pete. "I had to take a run down to the sports shop. I tried to get a neck guard to fit up under my helmet. The thing is just getting too small and I wanted to protect my head."

"Well, did you get one? They are important you know," responded Jim overhearing the conversation between his two teammates.

"No, I didn't," said Pete. "They were out of them and said maybe next week."

"That could be very unsafe, Pete," retorted Mike.

"Yeah, I know, but so far I've managed to make do with my helmet and I've been safe this far," answered Pete.

"Man, I hope you're right, Pete," replied Jim. "You are playing with your life when the helmet doesn't fit right."

"Jim's right, Pete," said Mike. "You'd better get one as soon as possible."

"You can count on that," replied Pete knowing his teammates were right and that he only prayed that he'd be able to play his game safely today.

The Gallagher's were all sports lovers and Pete lived for his time to play football. He enjoyed all his sports, but football was his favorite. He was so excited to be headed to this game they practiced so hard for during this early season.

Pete and his team spent the previous five days before this scrimmage game in what they referred to as "hell week". It had been a grueling week of physical conditioning. From early dawn before classes and again after classes until 6:00 p.m. every day each member of the team had a rigorous routine of calisthenics, crabbing, jittering, pushups, setups, and wind-sprints all in the effort to prepare each member's body to be in the best physical condition possible for the upcoming football season.

It was the beginning of the school year and the football season was just getting off the ground. There were so many games to look forward to and although this was just a scrimmage, Pete was still very excited about playing a game of football no matter where or when. It was in his blood – he was after all a Gallagher and it was in all their veins deep through and through.

The clouds were soft and billowy and the leaves were beginning to turn color. Perhaps the leaves will be in full color in Massachusetts? No, not yet, but the year was flying by. Soon it would be Halloween and the guys had big plans for the Halloween dance. This was going to be a great year ahead. Pete's mind was racing as he anticipated all the fun things that would be coming up. Summer had been so much fun but starting back to school his junior year was a time of anticipation of great things ahead.

Th3 mustang Pete's dad gave him was looking good. That car, that beautiful 1965 Ford Mustang, with its rich red interior and shiny black exterior sparkled and shinned with the brilliance of a new-minted coin. Pete had worked so hard to make this car a personal expression of who he was and what he represented. It showed his personality among its massive renovations. So many changes had already been made and lots more great things were to come. The speakers were changed to work with the lights. They now flashed on and off every time a base drum hit. What a charm. What a gift. Pete would be the hit with all the girls at Oxford. Not many of the guys had a 1965 Mustang. Pete knew this would charm the dickens off of Miss Lori Jenkins.

"Hey, Pete," said Jake. "You're a million miles away. What are you thinking about that has you off in another world?"

"I was thinking about my summer and all the fun I had, particularly at summer camp," said Pete. I met this wonderful girl and I've fallen in love. She is just everything to me.

"Hey, Pete," responded Jake. "That's great! That's really great, but you have a lot of things ahead of you before you get too serious about one girl.

"I know, but she is just the most perfect gal I think I have ever met," replied Pete. I hope that Saturday night my dad will let us take the Mustang out and I can show it off to Lori. She will sure be dazzled by all the things I've done to that car."

"Well, that's for sure," replied Jake. "You sure have worked hard on that car and any girl would be crazy not to think that car was just the best ever. Hey, you gonna take this Lori chick to the Halloween dance, man?"

"I sure hope so, but I haven't asked her yet," said Pete. "I think she'll go and I think it will be a blast. I hope she can come to next week's football game when we will be playing at home. It will be easier for her to get there and then you and the guys can all meet this wonderful lady of mine. You'll see, she is just everything wonderful."

"Man, you sure sound like you have been bitten by the love bug," replied Jake.

"I have," responded Pete.

She had the biggest blue eyes anyone ever laid their sights on. Lori and Pete had spent two beautiful weeks together at Silver Lake, the church camp that was home to many of the congregational youth across the state. Pete was in love. In his heart he knew Lori Jenkins was the girl he intended to marry. They had so much in common and loved so many of the same things. They'd have a wonderful family, a small house on plenty of land with acres of woods behind them. That wooded area would be home to lots of little animals and critters. Maybe that little house would be near the ranger station that Pete would be in charge of. Plans were being made for

Pete to attend college in Arizona and get his degree as a forest ranger. The anticipation was building the closer the time came. The time he would leave for college and return home to Lori with his education completed and time for them to begin their lives together. Lori and Pete would be so happy raising their two or three kids and sharing the wilderness and all nature had to offer.

He continued to daydream as the bus rattled along with all his fellow teammates. The game was exciting but the time spent with Lori at camp was so fresh – only a few weeks ago and he couldn't get this beautiful girl out of his head!

After the game, when Kingswood won, she'd be so proud of Pete. Saturday night was going to be a special night. They planned to meet at Friendly's, the local ice cream shop for a burger and fries. Maybe they'd take a ride in the Mustang, if dad agreed to let him take it out – just this one time. It would be a celebration of winning today's game. Dad didn't want Pete to use the car until graduation, but that was so far away. Pete was only a junior this year and still most of two years ahead before graduation. Certainly tonight if they won this game, dad wouldn't mind a short ride around town. It was so much fun to have his license and be able to drive now.

Pete had anticipated getting his license since he was old enough to think about cars. Now he had it and it was legal for him to drive! Wow – it was all so wonderful – this great life he had!

Maybe he and Lori would find themselves down Cherry Lane overlooking the water just in time to watch the sunset in the beautiful fall sky. Lake Pattanough was such a romantic place most of the year, but it had been especially beautiful this year as the haze of summer had ended and the sparse color of fall began to take on a new appearance. The bright flame of red and yellow hues shone brightly across the western sky where it met the gray blue of the sparkling body of water turning this lover's lane into a beauty of nature. The water that flowed gently down the mountainside from its natural spring sources that formed its own waterfall and would provide the perfect setting for Pete to entice Lori with his natural charm. Such plans, such wonderful plans. Only the best lie ahead.

Now if this awful headache would just go away. He felt very flush and his head just pounded. It must be allergies with the fall leaves changing and the heat. It had been an exceptionally hot fall day for New England. It would pass soon, Pete hoped.

"You okay, Pete?" questioned Chuck. "You seem very quiet today. That's not like you."

"Yeah, yeah, I'm okay," replied Pete. I just have this horrible headache that doesn't seem to go away. Probably the heat of this day isn't helping at all either. I feel quite hot as I'm sure everyone does."

"It sure is a hot one, all right," responded Chuck. "Did you take anything for your headache?"

"Yeah, I did," said Pete. "I'll be fine. Don't worry. Once we're out there on the field, I'll forget all about this headache and playing the game will work everything else off."

"We'll all forget everything, except the heat," replied Chuck. "We are going to swelter in all our gear and the heat of this day. It sure is a hot one."

"Yup, we will," commented Pete.

The trip to the Williston Academy was uneventful and now the scramble to get the gear unloaded and the entire team to change into their uniforms began. What great uniforms they were. The letters of the team were brightly woven in red across the front of the black shirts with each member of the team having their number brightly woven in red across the back. A team to be proud of and Pete certainly was proud of all of them. They had been together for four years and although there were a couple of newer members of the team, for the most part they had shared a vast amount of their teenage years together. They knew each other quite well and had shared some of their inner most secrets with one another, secrets that no one dared to divulge to another human being. Their bond was sacred and not one of them would ever break that bond. They were teammates forever, teammates to the end, a true school spirit that Kingswood developed in every young man who attended this upstanding school. They were proud of who they were and what they represented and today, as "the team" they each were a part of, they would show the world how team spirit, discipline, and determination would bring a winning finish and a start to the fall football games.

In the locker room was a bunch of other young men changing after a morning at the rifle range. Pete thought of the many times he and his dad had spent at his school and the special times when he had become an expert marksman on the rifle range. Pete also belonged to the rifle team at school, as well as having participated in the swim, basketball, and baseball teams, and was active in the lacrosse team. He enjoyed his practice on the rifle range. It was a fun sport and great when he and his dad had times in the woods. Pete hated shooting defenseless animals, however, and would make his dad quite happy if he just got the bottles all knocked down that his dad so diligently had arranged on the large gray rock about 150 yards across the meadow. Although dad had a very demanding job which took him away from the family, Pete cherished the time he and his dad shared, particularly early mornings in the meadow not far from home when the dew was still on the grass and one could hear the drop of a pin as the birds went about feeding their young, and the squirrels hurried to hide their acorns for their winter supply of food. Practicing shooting with his dad were special moments Pete would always remember. As he changed his clothes in the locker room, he heard the other boys talk about having to cross the rifle range to get to the football field. Pete silently prayed that all the participants in the rifle club had finished and that none of his team would be in danger of any stray firing.

Pete recalled those early mornings day after day when his dad would attempt to wake him early by sometimes shaking the tar out of him. After all Pete had newspapers to get delivered before school. Pete's dad would patiently gather all the necessary items that Pete needed and then dad's patience was over. He had better be up and dressed, time was wasting away. Pete could not be sure what scheme his dad would come up with to wake him if he didn't move out of bed now. Dad would then drive him to his pickup spot. Pete would load up his newspapers into his large canvas bag and slug the heavy bag over his shoulder treading through his route delivering his customers their morning paper. While Pete diligently delivered his 60 or so papers, dad would take his morning run finishing about the same time. The two would return home where mom waited with a hot and delightfully smelling breakfast for Pete, Dad and the rest of the Gallagher family. Before leaving on his trip today, he and his dad had done their usual daily activities of delivering papers and having breakfast. Pete remembered the events of earlier today and hoped that his comments to his parents would come true soon and this headache would go away.

"Once you are finished with delivering all your papers, Pete, I'll meet you at home," said Dan Gallagher as he dropped Pete at his paper pick-up point. "Don't dilly dally too long. We all have a lot of work to get accomplished today."

"I'll go fast, today, Dad," replied Pete.

"Remember that Stan has a game today too and we need to get everyone a decent breakfast before we all take off in our separate ways," replied Dan.

"See you in an hour or so at home, dad," responded Pete.

Pete drudged along as quickly as he could to get those papers delivered but he sure was hot already today. The summer had been a very hot one for New England and this September wasn't cooling off at all. Now he needed to fight the heat and get these papers delivered faster than usual. Pete ran to all his customers, dropping paper after paper at each stop. His head hurt a lot today – must be the heat. He made it home in less than an hour before his dad that morning – something Pete seldom did.

Stan, Pete's younger brother by barely more than one year, always was a bit ruffled at the edges at the breakfast table. Pete wondered if he slept last night at all, but decided no, this was probably just his normal look.

Jane, Pete's older sister, was quite the opposite. "Young man, keep your hands off that hair. You're sister has worked hard to look lovely," dad would utter.

Then there was the baby brother, Billy – born of another generation with a real different outlook on life, uncomplicatedness to everything. Nothing that was important to Pete seemed to be of any concern to Billy. Guess his generation will be different, thought Pete.

"Eat up everyone," said Ellie Gallagher now already tired from preparing a substantial breakfast for her family before they all scattered to do the things each were involved in during this busy September Saturday. "We all have a lot to do today, but you must eat a good breakfast before you all take off."

"Thanks mom," said Jane. "Everything looks great. I probably won't be home until late, so don't hold dinner for me. I have plans for the whole day and evening. Actually I have a date tonight."

"Again," replied Billy. "You always have a date. What's new"?

"Billy," replied Ellie. Be nice to your sister. When you are bigger, you'll have a lot of dates like Jane, too."

"Not me," replied Billy. "Girls are crazy. I'm never getting involved with girls."

Ellie and Dan Gallagher looked at each other with smiles on their faces, knowing full well that as little Billy got only a few years older his tune would change a bunch.

"You okay, Pete?" questioned Ellie. "You seem a bit quieter than usual today."

"Yeah, mom, I'm fine," answered Pete. "I just have this headache, but I'll take something and I'll be just fine." Pete didn't want to tell his mother that he was hot today too, because he didn't want her to think there was something wrong with him and she would, she was a mother. He just had a headache and that would go away soon.

All in all, however, this truly was a good life and Pete had been so blessed to be born into this family – the Gallaghers. These were wonderful times to recall and so many more to look forward to.

Today, however, was the game and he needed to focus on making sure all the padding was where it should be and all his laces were laced on his cleats. Pete focused on every aspect of his gear being perfect but remembered his failed attempt earlier to buy a neck guard. Pete thought of all the games he had already played safety and dismissed the idea that he would be in any unsafe situation now.

Pete was ready and about to leave for the field when one of the rifle team members approached Pete. "Hey just what do you think gives you the right to use my locker anyhow, bud?"

Pete was stunned. He was told to use this locker. He had no idea that he was intruding on someone's territory.

"Move it mister or I'll move you."

Pete stood still for a single moment and then decided to defend his territory. "I don't know what your beef is, but we were told which lockers to use and that's what we have done. You don't like it, go talk to the coach," Pete responded to his aggressor.

"Yeah, well I do mind it and if you don't move that stuff, I'm going to show you what movin's all about. Now hop to it."

With that the entire team came to rally around Pete. "Look here, punk. Pete's stuff stays and so does the rest of ours," Curly chummed in. "If you have a problem, perhaps you're the one who needs reminding."

With that, the red-haired bully backed off and sauntered out of the locker room. Pete was relieved that nothing more came of it. "Thanks, guys. He sure has a problem."

Pete was grateful for the support of his team but knew that his 6 foot 3 inches, 230 pound body would be no match for the slight-built bully!

The team hustled out of the locker room and up the hill past the rifle range to the playing field. Everyone was gone from the range and all the team members were safe. One issue out of the way and Pete was peaceful knowing his worries were for nothing. He was well aware, however of the dangers they all might have faced – just seemed like a poor design to the grounds to have the football field across from the rifle range. Oh well, that was a passing thought and time to move on.

The coaches were there and ready to begin. The stands had a fair crowd but not like the later fall games would be when a lot more of the fans from school would be present along with a ton of the local parents. Pete's parents were at a local game of his brother Stan's. The Gallaghers all loved football, well, all but Jane. Football ran deep for everyone in the family. Their lives centered on the game during the entire season. With three boys and a mother and father who thought that football was the number one choice in sports, Jane had to accept the nature of the activity and just live with all the football talk and activities around her.

The field was in excellent condition and it was evident that the maintenance department at the school had worked hard over the summer to make sure the field was in good condition for the fall football season. All these details were so important to real football enthusiasts.

The coaches were yelling. It was time to line up in usual formation. Curly was a big, burly sort of guy and their greatest linebacker. Doug, Mike, Eric, and Jim followed behind. Tom, Chris, Jake, Chuck and Tiny backed up the front lines. The first play was about to happen. The ball was kicked off to Mike, then the block – a 30-yard return for Kingswood and a first down. The balled is hiked and quarterback, Eric, turns and tosses to the halfback, Chuck. 10 yards – 20 yards – a 30- yard gain for Kingswood – a first down and we're more than halfway there, thought Pete. Tackle time. This was going to be a great game. Williston's defense just wasn't awake today. Kingswood was going to beat the socks off them. Coaches called the moves and the line was ready again.

The ball was passed off to Eric, down the line over Jake's block, and a touchdown for Kingswood. What a game. This was going to be fantastic. The game went on, and on. Kingswood 15, Williston 2. The ball was in Williston's hands now. Four plays and Kingswood held them – Kingswood was going to win this game. The ball was hiked. The quarterback pivoted and handed the ball off to Tiny, Kingwood's fullback and was making his way off tackle, running full speed ahead. Pete had to make way for Tiny to move through. He hurled himself in front of the opposition, to block and open the path for Tiny. One, two, ten on top – Pete was caught on the bottom of a huge pile up.

"I can't stand up, I feel dizzy," Pete utter softly. He fell once, twice. "I'm okay, we have to win this game," Pete whispered barely audible. The coaches and trainers came running. Pete walked off the field and sat on the bench.

Someone had hit Pete behind the head under the helmet. The place he knew was so vulnerable. The place where Pete knew a new neck guard for his helmet would have protected. Now Pete began to lose consciousness going in and out. "Time to get him to the hospital," responded Coach Henry Lang from Kingswood. "This is not a pretty picture. He's passed out again and I can't get him to come to again. Hurry, please! We need help."

The ambulance arrived and Pete, now totally unconscious, was loaded into the back end as quickly as the medics could move. The red light spun around and around and the sirens squealed loudly down the narrow streets to the small hospital in the next town.

Pete arrived at Cooley-Dickinson hospital still unconscious. Cooley Dickinson was a fine hospital, but they just were not equipped to handle head injuries. The medics brought him into the emergency room where Pete laid on the stretcher from the ambulance as the medics conversed with the attending physician.

"This young man has had a football head injury," said the young medic in charge.

"We're a very small hospital," said Dr. Blake, the attending physician. We are not equipped to deal with this, but bring him into the emergency room and I'll evaluate him quickly. However, you are not to leave."

Dr. Blake returned within minutes to the attending medics. "This young man has a minus five percent chance of living. He has bleeding in his head and is losing a lot of necessary oxygen. We just do not have the expertise to treat him if he were to have any hope of life.

"You must take him immediately to Hartford Hospital in Connecticut and don't waste any time. I don't think this young man will make it. He's had a serious brain injury and needs an immediate operation to alleviate the pressure on his brain from internal bleeding. Hartford Hospital is equipped for this kind of brain surgery with far more expert surgeons on hand. Hurry, please! I'll call ahead and they'll be ready for you."

Before the ambulance could return to their home base, Pete was again reloaded and the long trip was made to Hartford, Connecticut and onto Hartford Hospital where specialized physicians and sophisticated equipment were on hand giving Pete some hope of survival.

Chapter II

Family Awareness

The morning had been quiet on Pheasant Hill Drive once all the family had left for various football activities. The family had all gone off the various football games and Jane was alone. She was taking advantage of every moment. Their house was on a busy street in a very active neighborhood, but that Saturday Jane could hear every bird making their song as she sat on the patio reading her novel. It had been so peaceful having some quiet time. She thought it a bit strange that the street was so quiet, as though it was an omen of something that just wasn't right in her world. She tried hard to just engross herself in her book in between hearing all the calls of the wild birds above her head.

She sat on their patio for more than two hours and thought continually of all the family gatherings that had happened there. She thought of the many parties that her parents had hosted both inside and outside. The house had been built by her parents and finished only a few months before. The five-bedroom colonial home was perfect for their family with each of her siblings having their own rooms. Her parents enjoyed the large master bedroom on the first floor at the end of the hallway off the spacious living room. It had its own bathroom which was double the one she and her brothers shared upstairs off their bedrooms. That was always a bit of a situation when she needed to use the upstairs bathroom, but she usually convinced Pete to use the guest bathroom downstairs off the kitchen, and he was unusually accommodating during most of the times she asked – the only time she and Pete seemed to accept each other's needs. The formal living room off the dining room was large and spacious and was perfect for entertaining large crowds of people. However, during family time, they usually spent that time in the family room off the kitchen where they would all be enthralled in one type of sports show or another. Jane recalled all the samples of paint that her mother had looked at as well as wallpaper and fabrics for drapes. It had been a long tedious process getting the house completed, but finally they were all moved in and settled now. Now life could just continue as normally as any other American family.

Jane put the final touches on her hair. She felt so fresh from her shower and her new clothes just added so much to her new sense of womanhood. Now eighteen years old and approaching nineteen, the world held new hopes of a bright future. Graduation was over and Jane was looking forward to her college years; years of hard work in the theater and all it had to offer. There were so many possibilities, not just acting. Although acting was fun, preparing the sets, planning the new arrival of new companies in the local theater, preparing the community for their arrival were all so challenging to her that Jane knew she wanted a life that evolved around theater people. What she was going to do with a theatrical education, now being accepted at Yale, she wasn't sure, but the idea of working around famous and charming people was so delightful that Jane giggled as thoughts of the future flushed through her mind.

Mom and dad had gone off to Stan's football game in Milford, Connecticut. Pete had left with his team from Kingswood for the game in Williston, Massachusetts. Billy had gone with mom and dad to Stan's game, so the house was hers. Jane had planned to meet some friends for lunch and go to the early matinee. She had a date in the evening, so she needed to plan her day accordingly. Jane checked everything to make sure she'd just have to change a few things when she returned from lunch and the movies. Jane took one last look in the mirror and decided everything was okay. She could change her hair a bit later for her date with John when he came for her at 7:00 p.m. He was tall, dark and handsome and she wanted to look her best when he arrived. John had planned to take them to a comedy play being performed by summer stock in a theater by the shore about fifty miles away.

Jane came out of her thoughts when she heard a car drive into the driveway and a car door shut. The doorbell rang and Jane hurried downstairs expecting it to be Jill or Barbara, a bit early, but perhaps they were ready. Passing the window in the living room on the way to the door, Jane's heart took on an extra beat, as her blood rushed to every nerve in her body. There was a police cruiser in the front of the house. My parents, thought Jane, there's been an accident and I know it. She opened the front door to find two policemen standing there. Jane felt panic strike every nerve in her body.

"Is this the Gallagher residence?"

"Yes, it is. What's happened, officers?"

"Are your parents at home, Miss? Your brother has been hurt in a football game."

"Which one?" questioned Jane.

Looking confused and bewildered the officer responded, "Your brother, Pete. He's in the hospital. Are your parents at home?

"Oh my, no, well um, they're at a football game, no, well, um, they're with Stan at his football game in Milford," bumbled Jane as she stood dazed and shocked and confused. "Is Pete okay?"

"Don't worry, Miss, we'll locate them," said the officer. Now don't you worry. I'm sure everything will be just fine."

Closing the door, Jane stood in complete shock. Now what, what should she do? Jane's mind ran from one thing to another as she ran to the kitchen ready to pick up the phone, but whom would she call? She couldn't reach her parents. Pete, her little brother, the pain in the neck who was always peeking at her things, listening to her phone calls, and trying to see what she was up to especially when she had a date around was now hurt. Jane wondered how bad his injuries were. "Hospital, he must be going to a hospital," thought Jane. She needed to call Jill or Barbara. Perhaps she should go to the hospital and be there for him. But what if he wasn't there yet. "I'll ask Jill to take me to the hospital." What hospital? What hospital? Jane ran to the living room and glanced out the big picture window that spread across the spans of the sofa. The policemen were just pulling away.

She ran to the front door, leaving it fully opened, she screamed at the top of her lungs, "Wait, wait. I need to know the hospital," Jane yelled as the police car moved out of the driveway.

Jane ran and ran as fast as she could. She ran down the sidewalk when one of the officers yelled, "Stop, don't hit her."

Jane fell onto the hood of the police car. "Please, please, tell me if Pete is going to a hospital," she muttered in total exhaustion.

"Yes, Miss, yes. Are you all right?"

"Never mind me, what hospital? I've got to get there?"

"Hop in, we'll take you," said the officer. "Calm down, Miss Gallagher. Your brother is enroute to the hospital now, and we'll get you to him, don't worry."

Without thinking a moment further, Jane jumped into the police cruiser and trying to catch her breath. She was so grateful to be on the way to her brother. No matter how much he annoyed her at times, or teased her, he was her brother, he was family, and her family, part of them, and part of what made them all who they were. He couldn't be hurt bad, no not Pete, not her little brother, he just couldn't be.

Jane had crawled into the back of the cruiser without a thought that this was the area that all kinds of criminals sat with bars to protect the officers in the front from any harm. Now all she could think of was Pete. How badly was he hurt? Where was he? Would she get to him before her parents, and if she did, what would she say or do? Goodness, Jane had not given that any thought until now. She was only eighteen years old.

She didn't want all this responsibility, but where were her parents? But of course, they were at Milford High School with Stan watching his football game. Bet Stan was having a great game unaware of the family crisis. The family had been talking all week about the two football games coming up. Wonder if Stan's team is winning, thought Jane. They had practiced so hard in anticipation of this game with Milford. Why did Pete get hurt? Where is he hurt? Wonder if he broke his leg or his arm? Probably that's all it is and although that's bad enough and would take Pete out of the games for the season, he'd be okay and could play another sport during the winter and spring months.

"Officer, tell me how bad my brother is hurt?" questioned Jane.

The two officers looked at each other and the older officer decided to take the lead on this one.

"We really don't know how bad he's hurt yet," answered the senior officer.

"Well did he break a leg or something?" responded Jane.

"No, but I'm not sure the extent of his injuries, just that he is being transported by ambulance to the hospital here," replied the senior officer hoping that would stop the deluge of questions. She was so young and he felt she shouldn't have to hear this kind of bad news from him, but rather through her parents or the doctors who would be more equipped to handle the emotional stress this would have on this young woman.

Jane seemed satisfied with this information and could only sit quietly with her own thoughts as the cruiser navigated the roads leading them to her critically injured brother.

Pete was such a little monster when he was little but so cute. It was so easy being his big sister most of the time until he got to be about twelve. Then he became a pest and now he was lying in a hospital somewhere needing mom and dad.

"Mom and dad, oh, my gosh, mom and dad, officer, officer…" screamed Jane as she came to and remembered that her parents had yet to be told.

"It's okay Miss, there's another police team at the Connord/Milford football game in Milford informing your parents. You'll probably arrive at the hospital at about the same time," replied the junior officer.

"Oh thank you, officer, thank you. What hospital? You didn't tell me", responded Jane.

"Hartford, Miss. Hartford Hospital."

Stan had just made a touchdown – their son had scored for his team – Stan made a touchdown. Ellie was so proud of her family and thought of how fortunate she and Dan were. They had been blessed with four wonderful children. Jane, now eighteen, almost nineteen, was their oldest having been born while they lived in Seattle. Dan's company had sent him there to set up their branch of insurance companies in the Northwest Territory and in particular the State of Washington. It had been a fruitful endeavor and they had been able to enjoy a good life there. Pete had been born there three years after Jane. They felt that God had been good to them giving them a girl and a boy. Ellie and Dan had become very active in their church, a Congregational church, and both served on many of the boards. They had made a home there and had many friends who made such a big impact on their lives, and although they were on the west coast near Dan's family, they were still hundreds and hundreds of miles away from any family. Their friends meant a lot to all the Gallaghers and were included in so many of their social activities.

Just before the birth of Stanley, a year after Pete was born, Dan received news that the company wanted to start up some new business in Hawaii and asked him to head up the project. Plans had begun to make the move and two months after Stan was born the Gallagher family picked up stakes and sailed to Hawaii to begin a new life. They soon became very involved in their community in Hawaii and were charter members of the formation of a new church. After four years in Hawaii, Dan was asked to move back to Connecticut to the home office. Again the Gallagher family picked up stakes and moved back to the states, to Hartford, Connecticut. A more than a year later, Billy was born and the family seemed very complete. Now watching Stan play football, and knowing that Pete was playing his football game in Williston, Massachusetts, Jane more or less becoming independent, the family would soon all be on their own and not need mom and dad any more. Billy would still need them for several years – it was such a pleasure to have one more before looking to the future of an "empty nest".

As Ellie's thoughts of raising her children ran through her mind, she was aware of two policemen walking toward the bleachers. Wonder what is wrong, she thought. Someone must be getting bad news.

"Mr. And Mrs. Gallagher – Dan Gallagher?" said the officer.

"Yes, what's the problem, officer, am I blocking someone in the parking lot?" responded Dan Gallagher as his total body began to flush with warm emotions.

"No sir, your son Pete has been hurt in a football game. We need you to come with us. He is being transported by ambulance to Hartford Hospital."

Ellie Gallagher gasped loud enough for everyone on the bleachers to hear. Both Dan and Ellie felt as though their hearts had just been ripped out. This couldn't be happening. Not to Pete, not to their oldest son. How bad was he hurt – maybe it was just some broken bones? Dan Gallagher turned to look at his wife in horror.

"You go, Dan, I'll stay here with Billy and wait for Stan," Ellie injected.

"Excuse me, mam, but I think you'd both better come," said Officer Harvey. "Is there another parent who might care for your young son?"

"Oh my, he's hurt badly," cried Ellie.

"We really don't have any particulars, Mrs. Gallagher, just that we were to escort both parents to the hospital as soon as possible," said the tall officer.

"Now stay calm, dear, until we know what's wrong," Dan responded putting his arms around Ellie in a supportive and emotional embrace.

Jan and Mark Blakesley were sitting behind Ellie and Dan. They had been long-time friends of the family and Stan and Mark, Jr. had been friends all through grammar school. Jan put her hand on Ellie's shoulder, "We'll keep Billy and see to it that Stan comes home with us. You both just go."

An emotional rush of blood took Ellie by an overwhelming gust and grabbed her breath out of her throat. Dan, turning to the Blakesleys, picked up Billy's hand and gently guiding him to Jan, told him to stay with the Blakesleys. Dan turned to Ellie and in his usual sense of calm, "Come, dear, let's go. Let's just see what lies ahead. Let's just see how bad our son is hurt before we get upset. It will be okay. Just let's go with the officers."

The two officers escorted Dan and Ellis from the ballpark to their car. Stan had no idea of what was happening as he continued to be engrossed in his football game, and had no idea of the family crisis taking place.

Dan opened the car door for Ellie as they prepared to follow the officers to the hospital. Dan realized as he led Ellie by the arm just how much she was trembling. He felt shaky too but knew he needed to hold things together for her sake and the rest of his family.

Once in the car and settled, Ellie began to speak more clearly. Dan tried hard to focus more on driving than on his concern regarding his son.

"Dan, how bad do you think Pete is hurt?" said Ellie.

"Ellie, I don't want us to stress too much on the situation until we know more," responded Dan. "I will tell you; however, I am very concerned since we were both summoned."

"Maybe he has some internal injuries and they need our permission to operate," answered Ellie.

"We have to stay calm Ellie, or we will be no good for Pete when he needs the both of us in stable condition," Dan responded forcefully.

The rest of the trip Ellie remained quiet with her own frightening thoughts about what was really wrong with their son, Pete. She needed to pull on her faith now more than ever, praying that Pete would come out this catastrophe and their family would continue as usual.

At the ballpark Jan and Mark Blakesley sat with Billy and tried to focus on the football game that was still being played – where Billy's big brother was still working hard to score points for his team.

"Mrs. Blakesley, why did those policemen take my mom and dad away?" questioned Billy. "Are they in trouble?"

"Oh no, Billy, they aren't in any trouble at all," replied Jan Blakesley. "Sometimes policeman do good things too and help us when there are situations that require some helping hands. There has been an accident with your brother, Pete, and they are going to go and take care of things for Pete. Everything will be fine, I'm sure."

"Is Pete okay?" asked Billy.

"Don't worry about your brother, Pete," responded Mark Blakesley. "I'm sure he'll be just fine. There are wonderful people like those policemen who are helping your mom and dad take real good care of Pete.

"Are they coming back to get me after Stan is finished playing ball?" asked Billy.

"No, Billy," said Jan. "You and Stan will come to our house and we'll have some dinner and maybe we can find a great movie to watch."

"Hey, Billy," said Mark, "maybe we can even pull out the furniture and make a fort for a sleepover. How does that sound?"

"Okay, I guess," replied Billy with hesitation. "I want to see my folks and Pete."

"You will, but when things are settled down a bit more and we all know more information," replied Mark. "Right now, let's think about the game – look how close the score is. It's almost over and so far, Stan's team is ahead. That's great, Billy."

Billy wasn't sure it was great or not. He really didn't care about this football game at all. He was so concerned about his older brother, Pete. Where were his parents? What was happening to Pete? He couldn't keep his mind on this football game at all. He just needed to see his brother, Pete and find out what was happening.

Billy was very bright and considerate young boy at ten years old. He excelled in school and loved all kinds of sports. He fought continually with his older brothers and his sister, but anything that happened to them affected Billy. He always had them there. They were part of his family and he was lost when one of them was gone for any period of time. Now he was faced with a family disaster that was more than he was prepared to deal with at his young age.

The game continued for another half hour and Stan's team won by only three points. It was a close game and he came off the field exhausted from working so hard to score for his team. He was breathing hard as he headed for the locker room. He needed to shower badly as it had been such a hot day and all this gear wasn't helping any. He knew his family would be waiting for him, so Stan ran fast so he could get one of the first showers.

Once cleaned up, he headed out for the car where he knew his family would be waiting for him. He looked all around, but could not see the car or his mom and dad. As he walked further down the parking lot, he saw Mr. and Mrs. Blakesley coming toward him with Billy. Stan felt queasy – he felt immediately that something was wrong. This wasn't right. Why was Billy with the Blakesley's?

"Hey there, Stan," said Mark Blakesley as he neared Stan. "Great game! You guys did an awesome job out there."

"Where are my folks and why is Billy with you guys?" Stan said all in one breathe.

"Your folks had to leave, Stan and we will be taking you and Billy to our house," responded Jan Blakesley. "There has been an accident with your brother, Pete."

"Stan felt very weak and thought he heard them wrong. "What do you mean an accident? Where is Pete? What has happened to him?"

"There was an injury during his football game, Stan," replied Mark. "He has been transported to the hospital and your folks have gone there to see what is happening. We don't know a lot more than that, but I'm sure they will call us as soon as they know more.

"I want to see Pete," demanded Stan. "Take me to him right now. I want to see my brother. I have to see, Pete. Please take me there now."

"Take it easy, Stan," responded Mark in as calming a voice as he could muster. He took Stan by the shoulders and walked away from Jan and Billy. "That's not a good idea just now. Besides, we have to think about Billy. He needs a little calming time, as he just doesn't comprehend any of this just yet. We have to be patient and wait for news from your folks."

"I don't comprehend this either, Mr. Blakesley," replied Stan. "I guess you're right about Billy though. He's little and we probably need to keep his mind off this for now."

"That's my guy," said Mark. "Let's go to our house, have a bite to eat, and maybe we can watch a movie or play a game with your brother, Billy. That will help us all to keep our mind off what we can't do anything about right now. Okay with you, Stan?"

"Okay, Mr. Blakesley," said Stan. "Please don't keep anything from me. Please let me know whatever you find out about Pete just as soon as you know. Please promise me that."

"Okay, Stan, you've got a deal," said Mark.

The two males walked back to Jan and Billy and all four walked somberly to the Blakesley's car. It was a quiet ride to Jan and Mark's home knowing that their brother, Pete, laid in a hospital bed with serious injuries – or least they both thought they had to be serious to have to spend time with Mr. and Mrs. Blakesley. Why else would their parents have left them with friends if their older brother wasn't hurt very badly? How long would it take to know about Pete? Stan tried hard to just be there for Billy if he wanted to talk but he wasn't sure what he would tell his little brother – he was only fourteen and this was over his head. His brother, Pete, injured – how could this be? He had to be okay – he just had to be!

Chapter III

Her Beginnings

She was young, innocent and beautiful. At twenty-one years old, Nanette had lived a peaceful and loving life with parents who provided for and loved her and her brother, Jimmy, five years older. Their young adult lives had bounced around a bit but nothing like what lay ahead.

Lee and Ann Peters had made a beautiful home for Nanette and Jimmy in an old New England colonial home. Bought in 1943 during World War II, Ann and Lee had moved into this large home when Jimmy was only two years old. They had provided rented room to soldiers stationed at Bradley Field in order to help the war efforts and their financial needs. Ann was one of the best cooks in all of Connecticut and she often invited her "tenants" who were usually the wives of the servicemen to join them for meals.

After years and years of trying to provide a brother or sister for Jimmy, Lee and Ann Peters had made the decision to adopt a child. After several months of preparing for that decision, Ann became pregnant and gave birth at the end of 1945 to a bounding baby girl -- the only thing that Jimmy would hear of.

"I want a "baby sisser", said little Jimmy.

"But it might be a baby brother," replied Ann

"No, a baby sisser," said Jimmy.

That conversation was repeated for months and months and Lee and Ann worried if they were to have a boy, just how Jimmy would respond.

To their great satisfaction, they had his baby 'sisster' and Jimmy spent his life adoring her and Nanette adored her big brother Jimmy. Nothing would ever change the feeling they had for each other -- nothing. They would have their fights and disagreements but that would never change the fact that they were who they were to each other - "special in every way"!

The New England colonial home was large and spacious and offered wonderful room for all the people who lived in their home now and for many years to come. The living room ran the entire length of the home short of the stairway that led to the bedrooms. That room opened up into a well-lit dining room with windows on the south wall that extended from the floor to ceiling. That room became the "everything" room as the years rolled on in their lives. Then the dining room opened in a large eat-in kitchen that provided the social center for the family and where most meals were consumed. This room also opened to the front hall, the upstairs stairway and the generous living room. The openness of the home from one room to the other provided a perfect "tricycle" path for the two small children to go around and around from kitchen to living room to dining room over and over again. Each doorway suffered the scars left by the sharp corners of the tricyclist on their daily journey of "biking in the house".

Off the kitchen was a huge walk-in pantry that Ann spent a good deal of her life preparing family meals and baking up a continuous stream of Lee's favorite sweet things. On the other side of the panty and yet one more entrance to the home was what today would be called a "mud" room but in the days when the house was built was called the "ice room". This would have been where the ice man would deliver the ice for the old-style refrigerators to keep the produce, meat, cheese and other such items cold enough not to spoil. A continuation of the mud room was a laundry room which housed the "set-tubs" and a wringer washer at the time Lee and Ann purchased the home. The tubs (two in all) became the usual place for Jimmy and then Nanette to take their baths when they were little and a very fun time was had by both of them splashing back and forth over each other's tub.

As the years went along, Lee replaced the kitchen sink and put that sink into the laundry room. This sink was of the simplest nature for the times. It had a simple sink with a large side porcelain table attached. There was nothing under the sink as was the custom of the times. This sink stayed in the home in that very laundry room for more than 60 years.

The large house sat on a small plot of land but the family enjoyed every ounce of land it afforded them for their yard fun. Lee always worked several jobs but always found time to have play time with his children. He was the kind of father every child should have and every person should be able to pull on the good memories he provided. Lee was that kind of father - a one-of-a-kind.

As the years rolled along, Lee was not happy with the amount of land that was provided to his family having been raised with his father working on a dairy farm. Both Lee and Ann were used to spacious areas of farm land and although they had no interest in owning or running a farm, Lee was adamant that his home be large enough to not feel crowded. So they purchased a one building lot in the early 50's and then a much larger lot adjacent to that one in the late 60's. It provided Lee a place to garden and have this run for his hunting dog he so adored. After the purchase of his second lot, he decided to grow gladiolas and sold them by the dozens to passersby. He spent his winters preparing his bulbs and spring and summer selling his beautiful flowers while still maintaining his full-time job. Lee always found ways to provide a little extra money for the family so that Ann could stay home and be a full-time devoted wife and mother - and that she was.

During their early years as a young family, Ann had to devote a large amount of her time helping Jimmy with school work. In those days, there was little help for children with learning disabilities and Jimmy suffered from dyslexia - a learning disability that would haunt him for the rest of his life. This early intervention with the disability would prepare Nanette for learning how to live and deal with a "husband" and her middle son. Nanette was extremely patient with her brother and tried to help as much as possible to fill in the gaps when he needed help -- to her determent at times. Nanette did well in school and it was an accept practice to keep her accomplishments in tack so as not to make Jimmy feel bad -- something Nanette never wanted to do as she adored her older brother.

Jimmy quit school when he was 16 years old and began a lawn mowing business. He remained active in his scouting endeavors and became an Assistant Scout Master. His small business grew into a landscaping business and he acquired more and more equipment as the years went by. At 20 years old, Jimmy married and moved away and apart from the family.

Nanette was struggling for her own independence. She struggled under the protective and dominating eyes of her dear mother. A mother who loved her but had difficulties accepting that her children were adults and needed to make their own way in life.

At sixteen, Nanette had secured a part-time job in a local bank doing some old-fashioned type manual bookkeeping. After high school graduation, that job turned into a full time teller position. Within only a few months, Nanette was promoted as a Customer Service Representative but also having acquired secretarial skills in high school, assumed those duties for all six of the bank's officers. Her job responsibilities were heavy but more so were those imposed by her mother who demanded the daily errands tying her to return home every evening and keeping her from exploring other enjoyment for a young person.

Nanette had strong aspirations to go off to college in order to achieve a degree as a Certified Public Accountant. All those years of negative reinforcement, although meaning well, Nanette had become quite unprepared to leave the home she had grown up in and the protective forces provided by her parents, particularly those of her mother. How she loved her mother and father, but they were so poor. Her father worked as many as three jobs to keep finances on an even level while mom stayed home and took care of the house, cleaning and cooking, and raising her and her brother. What if she couldn't pass her classes -- after all she was such a slower reader and in college you had to read everything. Her decision to gain employment and not attend college came very quickly – there wasn't much use in battling all the negatives. She was convinced she wouldn't be a good college student even though with lots of hard work she had managed to stay on the honor roll most of her high school years. When her parents told her about the lack of finances available for her college years, she was more convinced than ever that getting a job would be better for the whole family.

Nanette continued what had started as her part-time job working at the local bank. She continued to accept the role of "good daughter" and doted on her mother and her needs daily. It was during this time that Nanette met Ken. One day while Nanette was still working as a Customer Service Representative, a tall young man came seeking her assistance.

"Hi, I need to open a checking account," said Ken Blake.

"Wonderful, come in and have a seat," replied Nanette. "What kind of checking account would you like?" Nanette was mesmerized by this young man and his handsome features. They continued to exchange the personal information to open his checking account in a very professional manner.

"Would you like to go out some time?" popped Ken in surprise to the both of them.

"Yes, yes I would," replied Nanette. She was not in the habit of accepting dates from people she really didn't know at all and she definitely did not know Ken Blake at all.

"There's one problem," he said.

"What's that?" asked Nanette

"I don't have a car," responded Ken. "I have come up from Florida and I haven't had a chance to get a car yet.

"That's okay, I have a car," answered Nanette. This was another sign she ignored. This man was not the sort of fellow her parents would approve of. He didn't have a car, but was from Florida. Why was he here? Why didn't he have a car? Where did he live? What was his background? However, Nanette took him on faith and made plans to go to dinner with him. Would she end up paying for dinner?

Nanette was stunned when she brought Ken Blake home to meet her parents before their date. Her father took to this young stranger like his best friend of all times. Ken was undeniably at a bad point in his life. He was 20 years old, divorced from his wife, had two very small children already, had no job, lived in a boarding house in a single room and had not met any friends. He was in most people's eyes, a "drifter". Lee and Ann Peters just melted around this young man and as they were the kind of people they were, opened their home and hearts to this young man Nanette had brought home.

Nanette enjoyed the company of Ken Blake for months trying to encourage him along the way. However, Ken worked at one menial job after another not making much money and thus his life stayed pretty much the same way until he was suddenly drafted into the Navy -- yes, the Navy!

Since Jimmy had married young, he was no longer living at home and it was just Nanette and her parents. Now at the young age of twenty-one Nanette realized she needed to change her employment with the hopes of freeing herself from the "small-town" atmosphere that tied her to her parents more than she wanted. She changed employment and found work in another bank twenty miles away. This was far enough to make popping home for the occasional lunch to bring the gallon of milk home for mom a little more difficult. She needed to make her own life and put some distance between her and her parents. A job a lot further away would help her to do so.

Nanette did well on this job and assumed great responsibilities. Within a year she was promoted to assist the President's Secretary, assume the responsibility of Secretary to the Investment Officer, handle the annual reports, and act as Receptionist for the Personal Loan Department. She continued her education taking every banking course available in the evenings. Nanette stayed in the city to enjoy dinner with friends or to attend her courses giving her the much-needed independence she had longed for. She began to get more involved in doing various activities with her peers and even occasional vacations away in between seeing Ken on her off time with friends.

Nanette made friends easily and had many who she enjoyed doing special things with. Nanette and Ken had become more and more serious in their relationship and it was a very sad day when Nanette had to say good-bye to Ken when he had been drafted into the military. He had given her his pin with the understanding they would become officially engaged as soon as he could afford a diamond ring. Ken was a year younger than Nanette and since he had already been married and divorced with two young children, it bothered Nanette considerably that Ken did not see his own children as much as she thought he should. But she was in love with him and thought that was his personal affairs. She needed to respect him for his decision to take his leave for visits to Florida with them or to Connecticut to be with her.

Nanette missed Ken immensely and wrote to him every day. He wrote her back often but as is typical with most men, not as much as she would have liked. She continued her life without him, made more friends, spent evenings and weekends enjoying herself as a young woman should. She thought of him constantly but knew she would just have to wait for those times when he could get leave and maybe choose to come to see her.

On a balmy autumn day while walking from her car to her job in the city, a handsome young Jonathan came up beside her. Jonathan worked in another department at the bank and they had shared other delightful times together at lunch and breaks. Nanette had been very active in the Order of Rainbow for Girls having now become an Eastern Star sister.

Jonathan had been very involved in his state in the Order of DeMolay and was now a Mason. These were the male and female versions of a large fraternal organization which they both knew and loved very much. They had dedicated most of the young lives to either Rainbow or DeMolay and now as adults had been very active in Eastern Star and Masons. They had a good deal in common and enjoyed each other's company. They spent hours and hours talking and sharing their commonalities.

It was this day when Jonathan asked Nanette to attend his college semi-formal dance as his date and she agreed – after all they were just friends and he needed a friend to attend with him.

Nanette was so excited. She loved to dress up formally. This would give her the opportunity to do just that and look very special and pretty for an evening, something she missed even when Ken was home. He never had the kind of money it took to take her out to a special evening that would require any dress up.

It was time to visit Aunt Gracie, her mother's spinster sister who still lived at home with her parents (Nanette's grandparents). Nanette adored her Aunt Gracie and it was a very mutual feeling. Aunt Gracie would give her anything within reason but always made you behave as a young child. It was a bond that would never be broken by the two of them.

"Aunt Gracie, I'm going to a college dance with a friend. I have a dress but I'm going to need some jewelry," said Nanette when she visited her Aunt Gracie.

"Oh, let's go take a look in my jewelry box," responded Aunt Gracie. The pair paraded upstairs to Gracie's bedroom and began to rummage through her jewelry. They picked out the perfect pair of earrings and then found a matching necklace.

"Now, honey, let's see what I have for an evening bag and a pair of shoes to match," said Aunt Gracie.

"I can't ask you for all that!" exclaimed Nanette.

"You didn't, I offered," said Gracie. "Enough of that. Which one do you think will go with your dress the best?"

Nanette carefully picked out a pair of shoes and an evening bag to match. She was a giddy young woman who had just had Christmas handed to her in April and squealed like a little girl. She was so delighted and Aunt Gracie loved to spoil this adorable young lady.

"Now, we have to find a pair of gloves that will go with the bag," said Aunt Gracie. She picked out a pair of off-white gloves that would accentuate Nanette brocaded beige cocktail dress and would go above her elbows to achieve the etiquette of the day when wearing a sleeveless dress.

"Oh, Aunt Gracie," squealed Nanette once again. "I'm going to be so gorgeous. How can I ever thank you?"

"You just did and that's all I need," said Gracie. "Just to see you so happy is enough for me. But we have one thing more to add to your evening." With that statement, Gracie went to her closet and pulled out her exquisite mink stole. As Gracie pulled out in view of Nanette, a scream that could be heard throughout the house expelled from her. Gracie smiled as she watched this young girl in such delight. She handed her the stole and helped her try it on. It was perfect.

"Aunt Gracie, I'm going to be the envy of every other girl at the dance," cried Nanette. "I'm going to be so beautiful thanks to you. Thank you so much for all this. Thank you, thank you, and thank you."

"You're very welcome, dear," replied Aunt Gracie. "Enjoy your evening and be just as beautiful as you are."

The dance was everything Nanette had hoped and she and Jonathan spent a beautiful evening together. Jonathan had been so pleased at all the effort Nanette put into looking so beautiful. This was the night that Nanette not only made Jonathan proud, but she got to meet many of his friends as well.

Before long Nanette and Jonathan were spending many lovely evenings together – as friends. Nanette was awarded the Carnation Degree from her local chapter of the Order of DeMolay and Jonathan attended to watch her receive this great honor. Important events found the two of them together enjoying each other's happiness.

One evening Jonathan asked Nanette a question that changed her forever.

"I'm not asking you, but if I were to ask you, Nanette would you marry me?"

Nanette was so stunned by the question she could not answer Jonathan and he was not asking her to do so. He didn't want an answer; he just wanted her to think about it. She knew then that she had fallen in love with Jonathan in a way she never would with Ken. She knew that as hard as it would be, she would have to write to Ken and break off their relationship. She got up the very next morning and wrote and mailed her letter to Ken returning to him his pin and a few other things he had left her. She no longer spent any time with Jonathan. Their relationship was now over also.

Nanette became very depressed over the next nine months preferring to stay in her room. She didn't sign up for any new classes that fall and stopped staying in the city for dinner with friends. She had been so hurt and yet she knew she had done her own fair share of hurting.

One evening right after dinner she received a call from an old high school friend. Jan's sister, Helen had a date for Saturday night and he had a friend who he wanted Nanette to meet. Jan already had a steady boyfriend but she talked and talked to Nanette trying to convince her to accept this blind date as a double date with Jan's sister, Helen.

"Come on Nanette, please double date with Helen," said Jan. "You need to get out and have a good time."

"Thanks for thinking of me, but no thanks," replied Nanette. "I just want to stay home."

"You cannot continue to stay home and think about Ken and Jonathan," continued Jan. "This is just not healthy for you. You need to get out. Look it's just one date."

"No, that's okay," responded Nanette. "I just want to stay home."

"Look Helen needs to find a girl for this guy and you need to get out," said Jan. "You have to get out of that house. Come on, it's just one date after all. Please, Nanette, please say yes."

"Okay, okay," said Nanette not wanting to hear any more from Jan. I'll go. Are you happy now?"

"Yes, I'm happy and I think you will be too," said Jan. "I'll let Helen know and she'll call you with the particulars."

Helen did call and gave Nanette all the particulars. She was clear about this blind date being just that, a blind date. She knew nothing about this guy.

Helen arrived Saturday night with the two guys right on time. As Nanette opened the door she saw Sam and Ean walking up the sidewalk and silently hoped that Sam was her date. He was so handsome, tall and lean. He walked so deliberately toward her front porch. He climbed the steps and reached for her hand introducing him as her date for the evening. Nanette thought her heart would jump right out of her chest. The place that Helen and Ean has chosen for the two couples to spend time together wasn't what she would have planned, but enjoying Sam's company made up for all the bad fibs of the "go-go" dancing and drinking she had to endure.

When they arrived at their destination (the "go-go" lounge), Helen came up beside Nanette very close.

"Remember I told you he was a blind date. He's yours for this evening but after tonight he's mine. Just keep that in mind," Helen said as she bumped her arm rather abruptly.

Nanette was totally taken back by the comment, but in her mind she knew that Sam was his own person. If Helen wanted him for herself, she would have to hope Sam felt the same way. She was pretty sure from the first meeting that Sam had eyes for her and not for Helen. Nanette was an attractive, slim, and sexy blond with flawless skin. She had just lost a ton of weight and was enjoying her new self even in her depressed state which was fast fading in Sam's shadow. Helen could not measure up to Nanette's looks at this stage of the game. She was at least 50 pounds heavier and was dark haired and didn't have the pale Anglo-Saxon skin that Nanette possessed. Nanette was feeling like she didn't really have competition with Helen where Sam was concerned.

After dropping off Helen and Ean, Sam brought her home. They were now alone for a short time to share more personal information. Sam had been married with a daughter and was now divorced. His daughter had been told that he had died in battle while he served in the military and Sam had chosen not to change that for her. Sam was ten years older than Nanette but oh he was so dashing. He treated her as though she were a queen.

"Nanette, you are so beautiful. Would you marry me?" asked Sam.

"You've got to be kidding," Nanette said as she openly flung her head back and laughed.

"I'm not kidding you," replied Sam. "I want to marry you."

"Yeah, sure," said Nanette never fully answering Sam's question.

The next several weeks Sam called Nanette every day during her lunchtime and saw her every night even if they spent the evening watching television with her parents. Nanette's parents were very puzzled with why he didn't take her out and away to be alone with her, but they were so mesmerized in each other these concerns were left inaudible. Every day, Sam continued to ask her again and again to marry him. Nanette would just change the subject and never answered Sam.

It was now late autumn and the days were getting colder. Sam was getting more anxious every day and couldn't stand to be apart from Nanette for even a minute. He had fallen in love with her from that very first night. She was so attractive, so sweet, and so innocent at the age of twenty-two. Sam asked her out to dinner and a movie that special evening. When they arrived back at her parents', he popped the question once again.

"Nanette, I can't stand living without you in my life forever. Would you please consent to marrying me?"

"Sam, oh Sam; yes, yes, I will, but before I can completely accept your proposal, you will have to ask my father for my hand in marriage. He will expect you to do that. He will also be very adamant about our children, if we have children, they must be raised in the Baptist religion. Can you deal with all this?"

"Of course I can. Anything that will assure we can be together forever, I will do. I will ask him tomorrow night."

The next night Nanette had Sam join her parents for dinner. After dinner, they all moved to the living room, as was the normal event of most evenings.

"Mr. Peters, I would like to ask you a question."

"What's on your mind, Sam?"

"I'd like to ask you for Nanette's hand in marriage. We are very much in love and I'd like to share my life with her forever."

"Well, Sam that is all well and good. However, can you provide for my little girl?"

"I will do my best, sir, to give her everything she will ever need."

"Sam, you know you are many years older than Nanette. You will need to understand she will want children. I hope you will want the same thing."

"Absolutely, sir. Of course, I would want children with Nanette." Sam reached out to hold Nanette's hand.

"Well, son, no grandchildren of mine will ever be raised in anything but a good Christian Baptist home. You must understand this if you think you're going to marry my daughter. And another thing, Sam, you will be married in the Baptist church. That's it. There's no room for discussion here. A wedding in the Baptist church and the children from this marriage will have to be brought up Baptist."

"Yes sir, of course, I fully understand and agree. Do we have your blessings then?"

Mr. Peters just nodded with a full frown on his face. He wasn't sure that was the proper thing for his little girl to do. Sam was so much older than her. He was of Polish decent; they were English. Would they be able to overcome the background differences? He was a carpenter. Would he be able to not just provide for his little girl, but would he give her the desires of her heart? He had so many questions. Did he do the right thing? The alternative would probably mean she would just run off and marry this guy anyway. She had become so independent in so many ways and she was a full-grown woman now.

Sam and Nanette were like little children with delight. They giggled and smiled and laughed all at the same time. Now Sam couldn't wait to get her alone and he hustled her outside to go for a walk.

"We have to go shopping tomorrow," said Sam.

"What do you mean, shopping," replied Nanette.

"We have to buy you a diamond ring," said Sam. However, I don't want you to see the ring, just the stone. Will you go with me?"

"Well, yes, of course, I'll go with you," said Nanette. "But what is the big secret about the ring?"

"I want it to be special and from me, but I want you to choose the diamond," said Sam. "Please let me do this in my own special way."

"Okay, whatever you want, honey," said Nanette.

Sam was so adamant he would not give Nanette her magnificent diamond engagement ring until Christmas. She begged Sam over and over to please give the ring, but Sam kept it locked in the glove compartment of his car and would not give it to her until Christmas, but Christmas it was. She gleamed with excitement and couldn't sit still for the happiness she felt.

Sam and Nanette planned a huge wedding almost a year away. She became enthralled with every detail of the perfect wedding. Since the Order of Rainbow for Girls had been such an important part of Nanette's life and this her very first (and hopefully only) wedding, Nanette chose to have seven of her dearest friends as attendants all dressed in the colors of the rainbow. Sam and Nanette were married on November 2, 1968 after knowing each other for not much more than one short year.

The happy couple moved into a small two-room apartment. They had a small living room with an alley kitchen, a small bathroom and a bedroom just large enough to house a bed, a bureau and Sam's desk.

"Sam, I want to have a baby," said Nanette. "You are ten years older than me and I don't want to wait. I don't want our children to have an elderly father."

"Sure, honey," said Sam. "I want to have children with you too and the sooner the better."

The first month Nanette was not pregnant she spent crying for several days. Her ultimate goal in life was to be a loving wife and mother just as she had watched her own mother. That was the way life was supposed to go, she thought. Then only two months after their marriage, Nanette became pregnant with their first child. Life was on the fast track for Nanette now.

It was a rocky time for the two of them. Nanette gained weight rapidly and over the next nine months put on over sixty pounds. At five months pregnant, she was forced to leave her job she now had with a real estate and negligence lawyer. Sam's own carpenter/building business was not doing as well as they had hoped. It was soon time to think about a larger place as the apartment would never handle all the things necessary for a baby. Sam continued to work hard every day and every night as he tried to get his carpentry business built up. Nanette knew he was working very late, but she didn't want to believe any bad about Sam. He was the love of her life and her baby's father. On the other hand, who does carpentry work at 10:00 p.m.?

In September they moved to a farmhouse on 200 acres of land, which they were able to rent. Sam's sister paid for the security deposit and first month's rent. Sam wasn't getting enough work to keep them financially settled and it was necessary to ask for help from Nanette's family. Nanette's Aunt Gracie came to the rescue. This was her niece and she was not about to see her and their unborn baby suffer. Every week Aunt Gracie would stop by and place a fifty-dollar bill on the table. Within minutes, Sam would have that money in his pocket and be gone. He'd come back drunk, downtrodden and broke. Nanette was challenged to produce enough food to eat for her and Sam. Sam became more and more distant and spent more and more days becoming drunk. His beer became more important than life itself. If he wasn't drunk, he was just gone, a situation that Nanette would come to learn much later that Sam was cheating on her.

Nanette was coming closer and closer to her time to deliver her baby. Sam decided since his work was so sparse and he owed his sister a family room, he left for Boston to build that room for Erica. Now Nanette was left on this 200-acre farm without a neighbor to yell to. There was no vehicle for her to use and no money to provide food for her or to pay the bills. Things had gone from bad to worse in a very short period of time. Their happy lives seemed so long ago.

Erica called Nanette almost every day to check on her and make sure she was okay. Erica was a registered nurse and knew this was not good for her to be so alone. She convinced Nanette to pack a few things and have her dad come pick her up, that she should stay with them while Sam was in Boston building this family room. Nanette swallowed her pride and went back to stay with her parents while she waited for the birth of her baby. On October 7th Nanette's water broke and, at the advice of Erica, she went to the hospital the following morning. It took hours for Erica to locate Sam and once she did, he decided to drive miles to their home, shower and change and then go to the hospital to be with Nanette for the birth of their first son. He only saw her for five minutes when they had to rush her to the delivery where she gave a very difficult birth to little Jake and the delight of his mother's heart. Her precious little Jake! He would fill the void that Sam had created in her life.

Chapter IV

Decisions and Reality

The officers sped through the highways and city streets escorting Dan and Ellie Gallagher in their own vehicle close behind. Since it was a Saturday, traffic was light and they were able to pull in and out of traffic, dodging cars and arrived safely at Hartford Hospital in less than 40 minutes. As soon as they arrived at the Emergency Room, the Police Officers tended to their vehicle and left Pete's parents to determine the fate of their oldest son.

Dan Gallagher was driving the family car following the police car in front, but he really had no idea where he was or what he was doing. The good Lord above was guiding his hands because Dan's mind was with his son and not concentrating on driving his car. He was very quiet and hoped that Ellie would not chatter all the way to the hospital because his mind was not there -- his heart was full of anxiety and worry about the life his son would lead if indeed he made it through this accident -- whatever had happened to his oldest son. Dan tried to keep his mind positive hoping that it wasn't anything serious. Knowing Pete had been transported by ambulance from Massachusetts to Connecticut because they needed more expertise. This accident was far more serious than anyone was telling them. Just what was the prognosis for his oldest son?

Ellie Gallagher sat in silence as her husband drove behind the police officers. She hoped he didn't start asking her a lot of questions because she was too upset to rationally answer him. How could she answer him -- she didn't have any answers. What could she say? She worried about their son lying in a hospital without his family with him in some sort of pain. She worried about what was wrong with him. It must be quite serious to be brought by ambulance from Massachusetts, but she didn't want to express those dangerous thoughts and feelings to Dan. She didn't want to upset him any further. She knew he was upset but he probably wasn't thinking about the ramifications of a serious injury or that this accident was as serious as she feared it might be. There was very little traffic, but it sure seemed like it was taking a long time to get to the hospital in Hartford where she knew her son needed them. Why was it taking so long? Couldn't the officers put on their lights and speed through the traffic? Oh, I guess their lights *are* on. Ellie wondered how long their lights had been spinning around and she was totally unaware? She must be in a daze. What was Dan thinking? Not now -- she couldn't carry on a strong and emotional conversation with her husband because she would just break down and cry. Not now -- they would be at the hospital just around the corner now.

The area around the hospital was a hustle and bustle of people coming and going. Cars coming in and out of the Emergency Room area. Ellie couldn't help but think there must have been a big accident but to their amazement the security guard told them that this was a normal Saturday at the Emergency Room. There were always things happening to people on the weekends. It might have been a bright sunny day, but to Dan and Ellie Gallagher it might as well have been a tornado hitting the very area where they were standing.

Ellie found her heart beating out of her chest, worried about what she would find on the other side of the Emergency Room doors. Dan steadied his steps as he led Ellie down the sidewalk from the parking lot and into the Emergency Room. The Emergency Room was packed with all sorts of people needing medical attention. Would they be left with all these other folks for hours pending information and instructions regarding their son?

Doctors and nurses were coming and going and the confusion in this large waiting room made their heads spin out of control. Where was Pete? Where was their son who had been hurt while playing a normal game of football? The white walls of the Emergency Room and the adjacent waiting room gave way to the reality of where they were -- in a medical facility, a sterile environment, a place needing to be kept spotless and as germ free as possible.

Addressing the Emergency Room nurse at the desk, "We are the Gallaghers. Our son, Pete was brought here from Cooley-Dickinson Hospital in Williston, Massachusetts. We'd like to know his condition and we'd like to see him." Dan Gallagher fixed himself squarely in front of the Emergency Room receptionist as he and his wife felt the life draining from their bodies in anticipation of what they might be told. As strong a person as Dan Gallagher was, he felt his body become very weak and his knees begin to buckle under him. He balanced himself against the desk and he tried to patiently listen to what the response would be from the person on the other side of this barrier -- a barrier that held them from laying eyes on their oldest son and securing a confirmation that he would be all right soon.

"Come this way, folks. Dr. Brown is waiting to speak with you. Pete has just arrived only about ten minutes ago, but Dr. Brown will speak with you as soon as he can," said the attending nurse. She led them to a private waiting room where Jane was already waiting for them. They all hugged, cried and sat in silence. Although the room was a small private waiting room, there were nurses, staff, and doctors racing from one area to another in frantic frenzies. Ellie couldn't help but wonder if all this frenzy was due to just Pete or were there others who also required speeding attention.

"Jane, have you seen Pete?" asked Ellie.

"No, mom, they won't let me see him or tell me anything about his condition. I'm just an extra person getting caught up in the trauma of the Emergency Room sitting here waiting for some word," said Jane. "I don't understand why they won't come and let us know his condition. They must understand how worried we are. Are they all so busy that they don't have time to tell the patients' families how their loved ones are doing?"

"I'm sure they will dear as soon as they have something tangible to tell us," replied Ellie trying very hard to keep herself calm before her daughter. "By the looks of things around here, I'd say everyone is very busy saving lives rather than worrying about telling us information. We just have to stay calm until someone comes and tells us something. They know we are here because they brought us into this waiting room and told us you were waiting."

"I just hope it's soon, mom," responded Jane. "Waiting like this is so dreadful. It's worse than trying to balance on a tight rope one hundred feet in the air."

"There, there, dear," answered Dan as he listened to the women in his life respond with the same frustration he felt too.

There were more people – maybe patients – coming and going; some in wheelchairs, some on stretchers. Ellie felt bad for them, but was somewhat relieved that all the scurrying around was probably not just for Pete. Maybe Pete's condition was not as serious as they were imagining. Ellie glanced at Dan who gave her the same body language as she was feeling. He was aware of all the commotion also and probably was wondering the same thing. Was there some large accident that included everyone and Pete was just a participant in a huge pileup or were all these patients individual cases?

Everywhere that Ellie looked there were signs of hospital life. The walls were lined with cupboards that housed various supplies related to those needing medical attention. There were bandages, gauze, tape of every size and type imaginable. There were oxygen tanks leaning against the wall outside their waiting room ready in time of need and vacant wheelchairs just waiting for the next victim in crisis. From where they sat, Ellie could not see any empty rooms, but where was Pete? Why someone wouldn't let them know about Pete. More nurses came running by in a frenzy holding syringes and blood pressure cuffs. Either there was some major accident or living a life in the Emergency Room as medical personnel must be very strenuous, thought Ellie.

The three Gallaghers were beside themselves. No one was giving any of them any information and all they had right now was each other to lean on. One or another began pacing the room waiting for word. The minutes ticked on by as though they were standing still. What were they doing? Why didn't someone come to tell them how Pete was? It was thirty minutes now and Dan Gallagher could not wait any longer. He left the tiny room and walked down the hallway.

"Dan, Dan, where are you going?" shouted Ellie not wanting to be left in this stark waiting room alone with just their daughter and trying to console Jane at the same time.

"I can't stand it any longer, Ellie," said Dan. "I have to find something out about Pete."

Seeing what appeared to be a doctor, Dan Gallagher burst out, "Please won't you please tell me how my son, Pete Gallagher is doing? We've been here for over a half hour and are waiting some word as to his condition."

"I'm sorry, Mr. Gallagher," said the young intern. "Pete is not my patient but I will find something out for you. Where have you been waiting?"

"My wife, daughter and I have been down the hall there in that private waiting room," responded Dan

"You go back with your family, and as soon as I can find out something for you about your son's condition I will seek you out and give you some answers," the intern responded. "Try to be patient as difficult as that is. It has been a hard day in the Emergency Room for the entire staff, but I promise I'll find something out for you."

Dan Gallagher returned to the tiny waiting room and reiterated the conversation to Ellie who continued to pace the floor. The minutes continued to drag along as they waited patiently for some word of their son's condition.

Ellie began to remember the months of carrying their baby son during her pregnancy. She remembered the feeling of her little baby boy kicking inside her, and how she and Dan anticipated his birth. Dan was scheduled to leave for a business trip for several days just as Ellie was due to give birth. Then the wonderful expected little bundle decided to arrive just in time to celebrate Easter Sunday and a day before Dan had to leave for his business trip. He would be able to leave Ellie in good hands in the hospital while he hurried his trip along and could get home to his new son and enlarged family.

There had been the usual ups and downs in raising Pete. He was such a determined little boy. He wanted what he wanted when he wanted it and that did not seem to change much in the last sixteen years. Pete had such a full oval-shaped little face with blonde hair and hazel eyes that just tugged at Ellie's heart day after day. He was a pleasure as much as a challenge. He knew just how to love his parents and they in turn bestowed attention and love in abundance to each of their children. How Ellie adored her children and her family. They were her life and now to be facing such uncertainty as Pete lay in a hospital bed. Then in the middle of her thoughts of her family, a tall strange man in a white hospital coat came into the waiting room.

"Hello, Mr. and Mrs. Gallagher, I'm Doctor Brown." I am the attending physician here at Hartford Hospital and have been stabilizing Pete since they brought him in. He has had a brain injury. He is unconscious right now. There is some serious bleeding in his brain and it is causing some serious damage. We have called in a specialist, Dr. Kirkland, who is far more experienced with these types of injuries. In fact, he is, in my opinion, the finest brain surgeon in the whole country. He is expected to arrive any minute."

"Surgery?" screamed Jane. "Did you say surgery?"

"Most likely," responded Dr. Brown.

"Will he live, Dr. Brown?" said Dan Gallagher as Ellie sat with her hands cupped over her mouth and face, afraid to hear the answer. She wasn't sure she could handle the answer to that question. Panic struck every bone in her body. Her son, their son, their precious son Pete, their oldest boy had just had a brain injury. What could they expect? What would happen to their boy? What would happen to their entire family? This was something that was going to affect everyone, not just Dan and her. How could she live through this? No, he must be mistaken. Pete wasn't hurt this bad. He must be mistaken.

"We don't know at this point, Mr. Gallagher. Every minute is critical but as soon as Dr. Kirkland has had a chance to review the case, he'll be in to speak with you.

Ellie, Dan and their daughter Jane sat in horrific silence as Dr. Brown returned to their Pete, his patient. How could this be happening to them? How could this be happening to their son, to their Pete, to their precious Pete?

"Oh, my Dan," said Ellie. "How could this have happened to our Pete?"

"I don't know, Ellie," replied Dan. "We'll just have to sit and wait for news."

"I don't just want to wait - they have to hurry up," Jane replied now panic stricken. "You heard him, time is precious. They have to hurry up and do something for Pete. You can't just sit here. You have to make them hurry up, dad."

"Take it easy, Jane," responded Dan. "We can't force the doctors to do anything. You heard them tell us that they are waiting for Dr. Kirkland anyway, and that he is supposed to be a wonderful brain surgeon. It sounds like Pete needs an operation and we'll be sitting here for a long time. So, just settle down, take some deep breaths and we'll all just have to wait, as hard as that may be."

"Yeah, dad," said Jane. "That is going to be hard to just sit and wait while Pete is hanging on to life itself.

That thought shot through Ellie like a sword and she felt panic strike her all over again. Her son's very life *was* in danger and all they could do was sit and wait.

Dan sat for a long time just remembering the mornings he had such difficulty getting Pete out of bed to get his paper route delivered but once out he did it compliantly and without much talking. He liked the money and used most every penny of it to fix up his Mustang – the car Dan had told Pete would be his when he graduated from high school. Pete had worked and worked on that car and put so much money and effort into making it his – his little piece of the world.

Dan reflected on the times he and Pete would just sit and talk about going off to college and what he had wanted to do with his life. Dan knew that Pete wasn't the type to ever sit behind a desk and push paper for a living. Pete had all he could do to get through his classes now and doing paperwork was real *work* for Pete. He liked the outdoors, the animals, the green things that grew, the birds and the critters that lived in nature. He was adamant that nothing take their living habitant from them. Pete just loved nature. Now this – this horrible accident. Would it rob Pete of his dream – his dream to be a Forest Ranger?

Suddenly, Jane remembered her friends and her commitments to have lunch and see a movie.

"Mom, I need to call Jill and Barbara," said Jane. "I was supposed to have lunch with them and go to a movie. They will be worried about me by now. I'll be right back.

"Go, honey," said Ellie. Make your telephone calls and don't worry about your brother. He's in good hands you know.

"Yeah, mom, I know he is," replied Jane as she left her parents to call Jill and Barbara to let them know what was going on. John would never understand, but she had to try. If he was upset, so be it; this was her brother and she needed to be in the hospital with her parents just now. He was the most important thing right now. Her friends, including John, would just have to get over any upset in their social lives. Pete needed her and she needed Pete.

"Hey, Barb, this is Jane," Jane responded as Barbara picked up the ringing phone.

"Hey, Jane," replied Barbara. "Did you forget our lunch date? What's with you? We went to your house, but the front door was wide open. We went in but it appeared no one was home. What's going on?"

"Oh, Barb," cried Jane almost in hysteria. "I'm sorry but my brother, Pete has been in a terrible accident at his football game. They are telling us he has a brain injury and may need an operation. We are all just sick about it."

"Oh, my heaven, Jane," squealed Barbara. "Is he going to be okay?"

"In all honesty, we really don't know right now," replied Jane.

"Is there anything we can do?" questioned Barbara.

"Yeah, could you call Jill and tell her for me?" asked Jane. "I have to call John and let him know also."

"Oh, sweetie, just go be with your family," replied Barbara. "I'll call them both and tell them. Don't you worry about your friends. We're all here for you. By the way, we locked the front door of your house. I hope you have keys."

"Thanks, Barb. Yeah my folks are here with me and they both have keys," answered Jane. "You don't mind calling John as well?"

"Absolutely not. You just go and be with your folks," answered Barbara. "They really need you more than we do.

"Okay, Barb, and thanks for everything," replied Jane.

"You bet," said Barb as she hung up the phone really scared for her friend and in telling John that Jane would not be available for a date with him. He was a pretty selfish kind of guy and didn't like things interrupting his life. She'd deal with him and set him straight for Jane's sake.

Jane returned to the tiny waiting room just in time. She saw another strange looking doctor, someone who had not been roaming the halls, enter the small waiting room. Jane came into the room just as he began to speak to her parents.

"Hi, I'm Kirkland. We don't have much time. I will need your permission to operate on Pete right now. He is in grave danger. However, you need to know that if I don't operate, Pete has little change of living – I'm guessing a minus five percent. However, if I do operate, he may never walk again nor have brain function of a normal person. You will need to make this decision immediately and understand what will lie ahead for Pete as he recuperates. I know this is a difficult decision, but his chances for life are not good the longer we wait."

Ellie was quick to respond, "Then operate doctor – now! Just do it! Save our Pete, please!" Dan just nodded in approval and watched as Dr. Kirkland made a very quick departure.

"Dan I hope we have made the right decision for Pete. He may never be right again. Are we prepared to take this on? How are we ever going to handle this if Pete is a vegetable?"

"Ellie, we've made the right decision. He's our son. He's going to live. That's what counts. He's going to live. We'll help him to recuperate and he'll be just fine."

"Mom, dad – is Pete going to be okay?" exclaimed frightened Jane. "Are you sure he should have that surgery?"

Dan Gallagher put his arms around the two women in his life. "Look ladies, we just have to trust the doctors now. Pete is in the best of care at one of the best hospitals in the nation. We'll just have to trust that Pete stands a chance to live because Dr. Kirkland knows what to do in this operation. We'll just have to be patient and wait as hard as that will be. A few prayers right now wouldn't hurt either. Only the Lord knows what is in store for our Pete.

The three Gallaghers sat for hours in silence not even paying much attention to all the noise around them in the Emergency Room. The silence for each of them was a way to cope with the thrashing thoughts of Pete's future and how each of them would come to grips with the changes that were inevitable for their family.

In the operating room, several doctors were assisting Dr. Kirkland as well as a staff of trained nurses, two anesthesia doctors to secure Pete's condition as the operation proceeded. Dr. Kirkland yelled orders back and forth to doctors and nurses as though he were a four-star general about to enter battle -- it was a battle, a battle for Pete Gallagher's very life and the quality that life might have for him.

"Come on team," shouted Dr. Kirkland. "Let's get this show on the road. Every second can be life or death for this young guy. Let's go, let's go, let's go."

"We're ready, doctor," responded one of the anesthetists.

"Well great -- and my team -- are we ready group?" said Dr. Kirkland.

"Almost, doctor," replied the nurse in charge. "One more place to secure.

"Let's go, let's go - this shouldn't be taking so long, let's go!" screamed Dr. Kirkland.

"We're ready, doctor," replied the nurse in charge.

"About time," said Dr. Kirkland. "Let's get the head shaved and hand me the saw."

The surgery began and the team began to flow like they had always worked together. It was difficult to assist a doctor you weren't familiar with or his style. Dr. Kirkland seemed demanding but in reality he knew that Pete's life was hanging on the edge and every moment of delay meant more danger for Pete. Dr. Kirkland continued to holler orders constantly but the team began to realize it was his own tension that created his reactions and caused his yelling. He, too, was nervous whether they would relieve the pressure and bleeding going on in this very young man.

The team continued to dredge on and on for hours responding to Dr. Kirkland's barking orders one after another. Each member took it in stride and continued to perform on cue, generating the results Dr. Kirkland needed in order for the next step to happen.

After more than five hours, they closed up Pete's head using a piece of metal to replace the bone they had to remove to enter his head and repair the bleeding and damage being done. They had completed what they could do for Pete Gallagher. The rest would be up to Pete himself. Would he respond in a positive manner to all their efforts?

Back in the tiny waiting room, the Gallaghers continued to wait for word on their loved one. The hours dragged on – one, two, five, would it ever be over? Would Dr. Kirkland ever return to tell them he would be okay? Dan tried to get Ellie to go to the cafeteria to get something to eat, but she wouldn't leave, afraid someone would return to the waiting room with news.

"Come with me, Jane," said Dan Gallagher. "We'll go get something to eat and bring your mother something back from the cafeteria. It will help to pass some time too."

"Dad, I don't want to leave mom alone and besides I want to know what the doctors say as soon as they are done with Pete's operation," replied Jane.

"Jane, no, you should come with me, now," responded Dan Gallagher in a sharp tone to his impatient daughter. Dan Gallagher knew Jane was very young to be dealing with these issues and it was her brother. They were as close as most siblings would be and none of the bantering between them mattered. This was her brother -- her brother Pete. Dan knew she was also very emotional right now and needed to take a break from all the long waiting.

"Okay, dad, I'll come with you," said Jane. "Will you be okay mom?"

"I'll be fine, Jane," said Ellie. "You run along now with your dad. It will be good for you to get away for a while."

Dan and Jane left to obtain something that would nourish them and also to get something for Ellie to keep her staying strong. Ellie sat on the small sofa and found herself dosing on and off in exhaustion. The tension in her head was tremendous and she felt a throbbing headache that just would not go away. Some sleep might be good. Maybe she would wake up and this would all be a dream, that Pete would come running through the door at home and ask what there was to eat, that he was famished. Then Ellie woke to a noise in the hallway and realized this was no dream. Pete had been hurt and was in very serious condition. She waited to hear something from someone.

"Mrs. Gallagher, I'm Nurse Kelly. Your son is in the recovery room and has survived the operation. He will be in the recovery room for many hours and you won't be able to visit him there. We won't know for a few days if the operation was a success but Dr. Kirkland is hopeful. He believes that Pete has a twenty percent chance of living. He is still in critical condition but time will tell more. Pete will be unconscious for some time, maybe even days. It would be best for you and your family to go home and get some rest. As soon as we know more, one of us will call you. Pete is in good hands here. We'll take very good care of your son. Please take care of yourselves and get some rest. There will be a long road ahead and you and your family are going to need lots of rest to brace yourselves for Pete's recovery. Go home and get some good sleep. I promise we will call you as soon as there are changes."

"Thank you, Nurse Kelly. Thank you for some good news." I'll just wait for my husband and daughter to return from the cafeteria."

"Certainly. Be comfortable and stay as long as you wish."

Dan and Jane were back in a few minutes with some food for Ellie and some hot coffee.

"Dan, Jane, the surgery is over and Pete is now in the recovery room," exclaimed Ellie with some excitement in her voice. At least the hard part was done.

"Is he going to be okay, mom?" shouted Jane in shear panic again. "He is going to be okay, right? Right mom?"

"We don't know yet, Jane," replied Ellie. "Time will tell."

"Did they tell you anything, Ellie?" ask Dan.

"Only that the surgery was over and that he will be in recovery for several hours," responded Ellie. "He probably will be unconscious for a long time, maybe even days or a week or so."

"Ellie, we ought to go home and tend to the other boys. They must be very confused as to what has happened to all of us. We need to spend some time with them also to convey all that has happened. This isn't going to be easy, but we have each other and we will have to lean on one another to get through all that will be ahead for us. So what do you think? Shall we go home."

"Perhaps you're right Dan," replied Ellie. "We need to spend some time with the other boys as well. We ought to go home for a while and get some rest too. This has been a trying day on everyone."

Now that they had received some good news, they were all more peaceful that they could take Nurse Kelly's advice and go home for some rest. They could return later that night or the next day when Pete would be out of the recovery room and then they would be able to visit him even if he wasn't aware of his company. Nurse Kelly was right, Pete was in good hands at the hospital that was able to perform an impossible operation and give their beloved Pete the chance for life – perhaps an uncertain life, but life.

Chapter V

The Grieving

The Gallaghers had experienced a very stressful day this September Saturday in 1969. A day which would be ingrained in their lives forever -- at least the 13th was a Saturday and not a Friday if they were superstitious people.

Dan and Ellie made their way from the car to the front door of their long-time friends, the Blakesleys. Jan and Mark had been busy calling friends to tell them of the football injury suffered by Pete. When Jill had called John to cancel Jane's date, she had told him Pete had suffered a head injury and that Jane's other brothers were staying with the Blakesleys. John immediately called the Blakesleys to let them know what had happened to Pete and thus began the cycle of friends rallying around to help the Gallaghers any way they could. John had surprised everyone with his concern for the family. Sometimes it took a misfortune to really understand a person's true nature. Many friend and family would surface now just when Ellie and Dan needed them most.

Ellie and Dan had taken Jane home to eat and get some rest while they drove over to the Blakeley's to retrieve their sons, Stan and Billy.

It was now dark out as Dan and Ellie Gallagher drove to their friends to pick up their other two sons and to deliver their news however good or bad it might be to their friends. The streets were quieter than usual, as if the world had stopped and everyone was in mourning. Did everyone know that Pete was lying in a hospital bed holding on to his very life? The night seemed darker than usual as Dan drove along the surface roads. Some houses had lights on but most were dark as the couple made their way along the quiet neighborhoods. The houses in these areas were eloquent with brick facade on most of them with most structures two stories, long driveways, and large yards. This was by all sense of the word, an affluent neighborhood.

It didn't matter now because a boy lay in a hospital bed holding on to life -- no amount of money could make his life the way it was. No one could help Pete grab life the way he did before today. It was true -- unpleasant things could happen to anyone. It was all in how each person would cope with those situations that made the difference. Just a short distance two more sons were waiting anxious to know about their brother also. As Dan and Ellie drove along, they worried about how Stan and Billy would react.

"We're going to have to face Jan and Mark and explain to them what has happened," said Dan.

"How are we ever going to be able to explain any of this, we don't understand what is happening yet ourselves," Ellie replied.

"We'll just have to be as honest as possible. We'll just be ourselves. We can only tell them what we know. Any projection of the future might just feed on rumors. We will need to be careful about telling only what we know until we do know more. However, we need our friends now Ellie, more than ever."

"Will our friends understand?"

"If they are truly our friends, then of course they will. It will be Pete that is going to have a tough time, if he even comes out of this. I'm worried that his friends will abandon him because he may be different."

"Oh Dan, I never thought of that," replied Ellie. "How are we ever going to be able to get Pete though all this?"

"We aren't Ellie," responded Dan. "Pete will have to get himself through this. We're just going to have to be there to support him, especially when people reject him. Let's just get him to wake up and talk to us."

"There's the Blakeley's house," exclaimed Ellie. "It's lit up like a Christmas tree at 11:30 p.m. Wonder what is going on? There are no other houses with lights still on anywhere."

As Stan and Billy greeted Dan and Ellie at the door, they saw twenty of the closest friends all gathered in the Blakeley's house. Each couple greeted them with huge hugs and offers of help.

Billy wouldn't let his mother out of his sight and Stan kept watching Dan. They were confused with so much noise. It was difficult for the two younger sons to understand what had really happened to their brother. How could they, they were so young and their parents barely understood what was happening to their child.

Jan took Ellie by the hand and led her into the kitchen. The counters were covered from one end to the other with covered dishes and bags of groceries.

"Ellie, everyone has been dropping by all afternoon with dishes and food for your house. There is more in my refrigerator," said Jan.

"Where am I ever going to put all this food," replied Ellie.

"Don't worry. We can put a lot of the things in my freezer and take them out as you need something. We'll keep the children whenever you need us to. Others have also volunteered! We're here for you and Dan, just ask."

"Oh Jan, thank you so much. We just haven't been able to absorb all that has happened. This is just so wonderful. Dan and I have to remember the other children in the midst of all this."

"You're right. Billy has been very quiet all day. He's more aware of the seriousness of Pete's injury than you might think. It seems to have really affected him a lot today. Stan filled up with tears when we told him Pete hurt his head and had to have an operation. He was holding back a lot but he too is real upset. It is going to take a lot out of the kids."

"It's all so overwhelming, Jan. Guess we'd better get the boys home. Jane is home alone right now and we should get home to her also. Thank you for taking the boys and telling so many people. All this - how will we ever thank everyone?"

"No thanks needed. Just take care of your family and yourselves, Ellie."

Ellie and Dan packed the car with their sons, and bags and bags of groceries and several covered dishes brought in by some of their dearest and caring friends. The boys were so full of questions all the way home. Questions that neither Dan nor Ellie were prepared to hear, much less answer.

"Mom, what has happened to Pete?" questioned Stan.

"He's had an accident at his football game and he's in the hospital," replied Ellie.

"A car accident?" question Billy.

"No, he had an accident while playing his game," responded Dan.

"What kind of an accident?" exclaimed Stan now more than just a question. He knew the game of football, after all he was 15 years old and knew a lot about the game. He knew that football injuries could be serious and his parents were avoiding the question.

"Well, boys we aren't exactly sure what happened on the field. All we know right now is that Pete had an accident while playing and needs to stay in the hospital a few days," responded Dan trying to keep the boys from getting too upset. Tomorrow would be soon enough to explain the details. They needed a good night's sleep too and getting them all upset over Pete would not be in their best interest.

"Will he be okay?" questioned Billy.

"We'll have to wait and see, Billy," replied Ellie picking up on the line of answers from Dan. "Tomorrow we will know more, but for now we know that the doctors and nurses are there with Pete and he is being taken care of very well."

The two boys looked at each other in the back seat of the car and knew that no more questions would give them any more details than their parents had already given them. They sat in silence the rest of the trip home.

It took hours to settle everyone down, get all the "goodies" put away before Dan and Ellie could finally take a deep breath and spend a few minutes sharing their worst concerns with each other. Neither Ellie nor Dan could sleep well that first night -- both worrying about the fate of their first-born son.

It was 6:55 a.m. Sunday morning when the phone rang. The folks of the Gallagher household were still quite asleep. Dan Gallagher began to stir as the phone continued to ring. He reached to answer the incessant ring.

"Hello."

"Mr.. Gallagher."

"Yes."

"This is Nurse Kelly. I wanted to call you before I left my shift to let you know about Pete."

"Yes, is he okay?" Dan responded now in a worried frantic voice.

"Yes, he is. He made it through his first night; however, he has entered into a light coma. That is not unusual with this kind of trauma to the head. The doctors believe he will come out of this coma soon. He is stable at this time. All his vital signs are good. We will just have to be patient for now."

"Thank you, Nurse Kelly. Thank you. Can we see him?"

"Yes, of course. We encourage family members to be present as much as possible with a patent in a coma. The familiar voices and touches can do a lot to help bring them back."

"Thank you, thank you very much. I'll get dressed and be right down."

Dan Gallagher's heart raced as he thought of his son, Pete in that hospital bed, physically there but so far away. So far away from reality. Would he survive? Would he survive and be normal? If he wasn't normal, what lay ahead for Pete, for the whole family? As Dan prepared to get up, he leaned over in bed to wake Ellie who was still very sound asleep. He explained the phone call from Nurse Kelly and let her know he was going to the hospital right away.

Ellie knew her place was at home just now to tend to their three other children and try to help them understand what had happened to their brother. Life would be different now -- this would change the Gallagher family forever.

The next few days were so stressful for Ellie and Dan. Pete seemed to stay stable, getting no worse but still remained in a coma. Dan took time from work at his job as a Vice President of a large insurance company. Everyone there was being so supportive and wanted to help. There was nothing anyone could do. It all depended now on Pete and whether his body would heal itself and he would wake up.

Dan spent hours upon hours at Pete's bedside while Ellie prepared meals and tended to their other three children. Ellie and Dan would trade off on those responsibilities so that Ellie could spend time with Pete as well. Ellie would relieve Dan so he could get some much needed sleep and vice versa. It was a tough time for everyone but most difficult for Dan and Ellie in their desire to be with Pete but also to be near for their three other children who were in such deep confusion.

Every time the phone rang, Ellie and Dan would glare at each other in wonder and fright -- would it be the hospital with bad news or good news. Most of the time, the calls were from more friends asking to help in any way they could. Often friends would take one or two of the boys so that Dan and Ellie could be with Pete together and have time to speak with one or more of his doctors.

One week after Pete's operation, the call came.

"Mr. Gallagher -- Kirkland here."

"Yes, doctor. Has there been some change in Pete?"

"He's still not conscious, however he is out of his coma. This is good news as I feel it means it's only a matter of time. When he comes to, it might be nice if he saw a familiar face. We have no idea what condition he'll be in or if he'll know you or your wife."

"We'll prepare the family and come to the hospital right away."

When Dan and Ellie entered Pete's room, Bart Ellington, the Pastor of their congregational church was sitting in a chair beside Pete holding his hand and praying with him. Dan and Ellie just stood silently in the doorway as Bart continued to pray. Without losing his grip on Pete's hand, Bart finished his prayer and then looked up and responded to the Gallaghers.

"He's going to wake up today folks. Don't ask me how I know, I just know. He's going to wake up."

Just as Pastor Ellington spoke those words, he felt Pete move in his hand and there it was - Pete wide-eyed and looking straight at Pastor Ellington.

Dan and Ellie Gallagher froze in the places they were standing. Their boy was awake and looking at them, but he was far away. He was not the son they had waved goodbye to only a few days ago to go play a game of football.

Ellie held her hand over her mouth afraid her feelings would show and scare Pete even more. Dan could not bear to see his son this way -- just a blank stare at him as though he was a total stranger. Dan turned and left the hospital room in order to gain composure for his son and wife. He was the head of the household. He had to hold things together for the sake of all of them.

Ellie moved closer to the bed as Pastor Ellington put Pete's hand into Ellie's. This was her son, their son. This was Pete's hand but the hallowed look in his eyes scared Ellie and she hoped it didn't show. Pete looked at his mother but made no noise or gave any sign of recognition. Ellie's heart was broken all over again. Where was her son, her beautiful baby boy?

Dan Gallagher returned to the hospital room and moved beside his wife. Pete looked at his father and made several very loud noises. It was now Ellie's turn to lose her emotional stability. She put Pete's hand in Dan's and moved across the room with her back to her son and husband.

"Pete, it's dad," said Dan. "Can you understand me, son?"

Pete made several more very loud noises as his eyes grew wider. He looked like the most frightened child Dan had ever looked at. His son lay in a hospital bed with his head wrapped in bandages but unable to communicate with anyone.

"Pete, I'm here," said Dan. "I won't leave you, son. Don't be frightened. We're all going to take care of you." Dan put his whole arm around Pete's arm and held him tightly.

Pete looked from his father to his mother and then to Pastor Ellington. They all smiled at Pete and suddenly there appeared more peace over his face. Within minutes Pete fell asleep again.

Dan and Ellie looked at each other and then to Pastor Ellington.

"We're all going to have to say a lot of prayers for Pete," said Pastor Ellington. He's very frightened. I'm sure he doesn't understand what has happened. If he can't remember anything, it is making him all the more frightened."

"What can we do for him, Pastor?" questioned Dan.

"Just pray Dan and you too Ellie," replied Pastor. "Just pray. The greatest physician in the entire universe is Jesus Christ himself. Ask for his help."

"Thank you, Pastor," said Ellie. "I'm so glad you were here when he woke up. He seemed to know who you are."

"Maybe, Ellie, just maybe," responded the Pastor.

The days ahead were lots more of the same and concern mounted for Pete's parents wondering if he would speak or recognize them.

Pete received all kinds of cards and letters from friends and classmates but few came for a second visit. Pete had changed and his peers had a hard time accepting the new Pete. While he was still trying to learn how to walk again, his old friends and classmates where enjoying the normal teenage years of going to parties, football games, classes and dates. His own family had a hard time accepting the new Pete.

"Ellie, you have to stop trying so hard to find and make the old Pete come back," said Doctor Faulkner.

"But doctor, I just want to see my son again. Where is the Pete that used to live at our house? I want him to walk through the door and demand dinner. I want him to drop his hat and coat and have me yell at him for not hanging it up. I want him to run around getting his football gear ready for his next game and to see him lifting his weights to stay in shape. I just want my son back," Ellie responded in sheer frustration and grief.

"Ellie you need to mentally bury the old Pete. You now have a new son. One who has been given to you with lots of limitations. You are going to have to accept that the old Pete is dead but this new Pete needs you more than the old one ever did or ever would. This Pete is hurting inside and out and needs his mother, his caring and compassionate mother. You need to love this Pete like you've never loved before - he needs you Ellie."

"Just how am I supposed to do that, doctor?" cried Ellie.

"I know it is difficult, but Pete's rehabilitation depends on it and I know you can do this -- you're his mother. You have to for Pete's sake," responded Dr. Faulkner.

Ellie had no idea how she was supposed to say goodbye to the old Pete when the person in the hospital looked like her son -- he just didn't act like her son. She cried and grieved a lot over the next several weeks and month. It took Ellie a long time to come to terms with the new person she now had as a son. Her son had not died but had changed into another person -- a person she had to get to know. After all, he was still the person who she gave birth to and the person she had to learn a new kind of compassion for.

After nearly three months in the hospital, Pete was ready to be moved to the continuing care unit for more intensive rehabilitation. Although this unit was part of the hospital, it ran as an independent facility that was more equipped to help Pete learn to walk, talk, read and write. Pete had a lot of learning ahead of him. There was no easy fix for this young man and his family

Every day brought a new challenge for Pete and his family. He was being taught how to live the basic parts of life all over again. He had therapy to learn to walk and to talk just as though he was beginning life all over again. After all he was! On alternate days, Pete had studies where he learned how to read and write again. He was being challenged every day for new things and having a very difficult time remembering what he had been taught from the day before. There were more teachers, aids, and nurses trying to help Pete regain the basic skills and yet Pete had difficulty even remembering each person, their names, or what their responsibility was toward him. They could teach him all they wanted, but Pete was having a lot of problems retaining and learning all these new concepts at once.

He felt and showed anger often and that was not helping him. Pete had his brain injury long before there had been any extensive studying about injuries to the brain. So when he demonstrated anger toward his instructors, they automatically assumed he had a "mental" problem and would isolate him. As the years went by and more research was done, including the amazing things that Pete learned after his injury, looking back this was a period in his life when he was being bombarded with more things than his brain was equipped to handle at the time. It took years for his brain to catch up with the idea that part of it was dead and the other parts had to increase its capacity, a fact that did partially indeed happen.

Mentally, Pete had a hard time accepting this new body. At first he believed he would regain everything and be his old self. As more and more time passed, however, Pete realized he would never be his old self again. He would never go to college. He would never have the life he planned.

Lori Higgins came to see him once and never returned. Pete was so hurt. He had loved her so much. All that was over. Now what? What would become of him, Pete thought. Would he ever be able to get married and have a family?

Pete fell into a huge depression and didn't want to continue all this therapy. It took lots and lots of pushing and coaxing to get him through his routine every day.

His outbursts and acting out became a problem as Pete continued to demonstrate irrational behavior to everyone around him. He would verbally abuse anyone who got near him. The verbal assaults were bad enough but then Pete began to demonstrate physical assaults, which landed him in restraints. Pete spent a lot of time being restrained as the doctors worked constantly to help him with various medications to subdue his personality traits now being exhibited in negative manners.

The episodes continued to get worse and worse every day. The doctors were very frustrated as they attempted to change and rework various medications to help Pete. The decision was made to move Pete to a mental institution where they might be more prepared to handle him and to give Pete the kind of help he needed.

Although Dan and Ellie knew the decision to move Pete to the Institute for Living was the correct one, they continued to grieve over the loss of the son they once knew. The very rambunctious little boy and the vivacious teenager with the energy of three people was gone. In his place was the angry, frustrated and impatient 'new' son trying hard to understand why life dealt him such a raw deal.

Now instead of bringing home a normal well-adjusted son from surgery, they would now be faced with yet more hospitalization, only now for all the emotional and mental stress Pete was living with. Was this ordeal ever going to settle down? Would their family ever live their lives the way other families did? Dan and Ellie continued to remember the words of Pastor Ellington – "pray, just pray," and that they did every day!

Chapter VI

Reality, Rehabilitation and The Family

Pete lay unconscious for several days as his family, friends, doctors, and pastor waited impatiently praying that Pete would come to and be okay. Pete, however, was going through a different experience.

He was very aware of a beautiful white light in front of him and he walked toward that light. It was the most beautiful light he had ever experienced and he felt a calming spirit fall over him the farther he walked. Just as Pete began to walk uphill following the stunning and majestic light, a man dressed in a long white robe seemed to appear from nowhere.

"Hello, Pete", said this stranger in the white robe.

"How do you know my name?" said Pete.

"I know everyone's name, but that's not important. It is not your time, Pete and we need to turn around now and take you back," said the white-robed stranger.

"Back to where?" said Pete. "I don't understand."

"You will, Pete," responded the stranger. "Let's walk together and think of all the wonderful people who love you and how much they are missing you."

"Why would they be missing me?" exclaimed Pete. "You are talking in circles."

"Come Pete. We'll talk of pleasant things as we walk back."

The stranger and Pete talked about Pete's family, his school, thoughts about his future, and his beloved game of football. In no time, Pete's new friend, whom he never did find out his name, had left him. Pete could hear lots of voices around him, but he couldn't talk to anyone. He couldn't make his mouth work or his eyes open. He could hear more voices, but they didn't make any sense. This feeling stayed with Pete for what to him felt like eternity. He *so* wanted to understand and to tell someone what he was thinking but nothing worked. Then slowly Pete's eyes began to open. Pete eyes first fell on his Pastor, Pastor Bart Ellington standing beside him very close.

"Hey there, Pete," said Pastor Ellington. "You've been out of it for some time. How are you doing my boy?"

Pete just stared at the Pastor hearing strange sounds, but not understanding any of what he heard.

"Can you hear me, Pete?" asked Pastor Ellington.

Again, Pete just stared at his Pastor. He knew who Pastor Ellington was, but Pete could not make his words come out of his mouth and whatever noise Pastor Ellington was making made no sense.

Within minutes both Dan and Ellie Gallagher were beside Pete trying to talk to their son, but getting no more response than Pastor Ellington. Pete had no idea who this man and woman were but something seemed familiar with them -- more with the man than the woman. They were babbling away and he had no idea what they were saying. None of it made any sense.

There were other people in the room, but Pete was not sure who they were either. He couldn't remember anyone looking like these people. "I can't say the words. Why don't they understand me?" thought Pete.

Pete was uttering noise, his eyes were wide awake and people all over his room now were talking to him. He couldn't understand anyone nor could he make them understand him. What was going on? Pete's mind was racing in all directions. Where was he? What had happened? Why couldn't he understand these people or they understand him?

It took Pete more than a week to make words sound like words. He had a terrible time understanding what everything was that the doctors and nurses kept asking him. It took a long time for Pete to understand what a toothbrush was, or what a washcloth was much less using these things. Comb his hair -- what was that? The things that people took for granted day in and day out were so foreign now to Pete. It was so frustrating for Pete. He was starting life all over again at age sixteen.

Over the next several days there were all sorts of people visiting Pete and making these crazy noises but making no sense to Pete. Doctors and nurses were at Pete's side most of every day helping him with life's basic tasks. His legs did not work at all. It was thought that perhaps his length of time in bed had created some inability for Pete to use his legs. It was not long before the doctors realized that Pete was paralyzed on his left side and it would take some time to get all these functions working again, if ever!

Pete was so confused at all the things they kept bringing him. He had no idea what these special small tools were, like a comb or a toothbrush, much less how to use them for the intended purposes. Wonderful aids brought meals with utensils and Pete had more confusion – what was all this stuff?

It would take Pete more than two months in Hartford Hospital to just relearn how to use these things. He now needed to physically function, including learning to walk the best that he could, and to relearn how to use the bathroom, to shower, to comb his hair, and to brush his teeth. All the things that seemed to come so naturally to those around him were mountainous tasks for Pete.

Pete was very fortunate, however, that in about a week from the time he first saw Pastor Ellington he began to understand a few words. It would be a long learning process to understand what people were trying to tell him and to learn how to express himself. Speech would be another thing to relearn at sixteen years old, but the doctors were not hopeful the speech would return to a normal level.

It would be frustrating for his friends and family to want him to know how to do things and use the tools so necessary to living life. It would be a very long tedious journey of new beginnings for Pete Gallagher and his family. The next several months put all the Gallaghers through a tough test of endurance and courage.

Pete's biggest challenge was learning how to live with his new self, a self he was very uncomfortable and angry with.

Everything Pete encountered was strange with so many strange people around. He knew his parents and yet he didn't. They seemed familiar but he couldn't remember the things of his childhood and where they really fit into his life. There was something about them that seemed real and other things that made him feel like he had just met them.

After three months, Pete would be faced with more new stuff and more new people. He was now going to move to the Institute for the Mentally Challenged.

"Hello, Pete. I'm Dr. Monica Levine. I'm a psychologist. I work at the hospital some of the time and at the Institute some of the time. I'm going to help you understand yourself and how to live with the new person you are now."

Pete was aware of the Institute, as he had been told he would have to spend some time living there after he finished his rehabilitation at the hospital. All Pete could think of was that everyone considered him "crazy" now!

"I don't need a shrink," answered Pete with tremendous anger.

"Oh, I think you do. You know, Pete, we all benefit from talking about our feeling particularly with folks we care about."

"Yeah, well I don't care about you and I don't have any feelings to talk about."

Pete didn't like Dr. Levine or the Institute for the Mentally Challenged. It was dark and dingy with brick or cement walls. He was so full of anger that he couldn't see the wonderful blooming flowers of early spring on the vast rolling hills of lush green grass that spread across acres and acres of the campus. There were over ten buildings, which comprised the campus at the Institute. Some of the buildings housed patients, others doctors' offices, and still others contained multiple rooms used for various therapies from art classes to physical therapy. Harboring so much anger and bitterness, Pete just hated them all, every last one of them. He resented his life being turned upside down and the changes now for his future – his plans all gone now, gone and never to return!

While at the Institute for the Mentally Challenged, still other combinations and doses of medications were administered in order to help Pete with his outbursts and his episodes of acting out. At the Institute, however, Pete was not only held in restraints a good portion of the time but when he experienced one of his episodes, he would be put in an isolation room with little clothing and/or covers and then covered in cold packs, a treatment which was at the time thought to help to calm the nervous system. Pete never forgot these treatments – they were intense and uncomfortable.

Pete was angry, so angry that his life wasn't returning to normal. All the doctors, nurses, and family kept assuring him he would adjust to his new life. That was just not so; he felt he would never adjust. Pete was now seventeen years old and all his hopes and plans had been shattered in one split second.

"We all have feelings, Pete. Sometimes when we have anger, we don't let out our true feelings out," explained Dr. Levine.

"You can't make me talk about my *feelings* if I don't want to."

"You're right, Pete. I can't. Suppose we talk about my feelings, then."

Pete hated these sessions with Dr. Levine. After all he didn't need to hear about how she felt every day. These were his sessions, yet he had to endure listening to this nonsense every day for weeks and weeks and weeks.

About twelve weeks into their sessions, Pete finally told her how he felt. Dr. Levine had patiently waited for this day. The day they could finally begin Pete's therapy.

They would talk about his new limitations, his anger about his accident, and how his friends didn't want to be in his presence. They talked about his parents and how they seemed different in how they treated him; how he felt like a baby – after all he wasn't a baby, he was seventeen years old. He was a man now or at least he thought of himself as a man. He was as big as the other men in his life and he had to shave every day now – he was a man. Dr. Levine and Pete talked about how he felt about his brothers and sister, and Pete shared his anger about how they treated him as less than human – he was still a human being, couldn't they see that?

Dr. Levine and Pete spent hours, days, weeks and months talking about the same issues over and over again. Pete thought she just did not hear him – he had to repeat himself so many times. What was wrong with her?

After more than six months of constant psychological treatment with sessions with Dr. Levine, it was apparent that real improvement had been made. Pete and his entire attitude toward life had changed – for the better! However, he was still living at the Institute and she wasn't sure how Pete would do if she were to release him to go home and live with his parents.

After working with Pete for a few months at the hospital and now six months at the Institute, Dr. Levine had consulted a social vocational therapist from the Department of Vocational Rehabilitation, which later became known as the Department of Mental Retardation, a new handle that would haunt Pete for the rest of his life. Pete was not mentally retarded but in the early 1970's there were no specialized agencies in place to help those who had suffered a brain injury. This was the best that Dr. Levine could do to help Pete begin to regain life in the community – her ultimate goal.

Through Judy Collins, who became a true friend to Pete Gallagher, Pete had slowly been introduced into a part-time employment situation. Now after several months, the team of doctors from both Hartford Hospital and the Institute for the Mentally Challenged, Dr. Monica Levine, Judy Collins and Dan and Ellie Gallagher prepared a new plan for Pete to help him continue to a productive environment that would prepare him for what his new life might be like as an active member of society.

Pete got his first job while still living at the Institute working with Goodwill Industries learning how to fix small appliances. He needed constant reminders of the tasks he had learned from as short as an hours ago and thus he was placed in what is known as 'supportive employment' where he had a job coach who would patiently remind him over and over and over of his job responsibilities.

Just learning how to take the bus from Hartford, Connecticut to Springfield, Massachusetts more than twenty-five miles one way became a large milestone for Pete. The daily trip was another task to achieve for Pete and one he had to remember – his toughest challenge and one that would haunt him forever. Pete would need to learn every shortcut and trick available to help him to jog his memory on those occasions that most human beings find part of everyday life.

"What am I supposed to do today?" asked Pete early Monday morning

"You are going to fix this appliance the same way I showed you on Friday," responded Charlie Fox, Pete's first job coach.

"Yeah, well you didn't show me how to fix this thing on Friday," responded Pete.

"Sure, I did Pete, but let's go over it again."

The days and the hours were the same, repeating the tasks over and over again, but Charlie had the patience of a saint and continued to show Pete how to do the same tasks over and over again. This was a scene that

Pete would continue to play out for the rest of his working career in one form or another – his memory would improve but never be perfect again. The days of frustration led to fatigue for Pete Gallagher and he became very discouraged many days. The one thing that kept Pete going was his commitment to his faith in God above to change his life for the better. His one true hope was to have a girlfriend that would marry him and together they would raise a family. He prayed every day to the Lord that this desire of his heart would come to pass one day.

Pete made progress but it was slow. During his time at the Institute, Pete was allowed to go home on weekends which proved to have another set of its own problems – now learning how to get along with his family and friends now that everyone saw him as different and Pete knew it.

During this time, Pete was reintroduced to a psychiatrist who helped him earlier, Dr. Theodore Harkins. Pete saw Dr. Harkins at the Institute weekly for several weeks and it was Dr. Harkins who was so instrumental in finding the right medication to help Pete remain calm and in control of his life. Pete became very fond of Dr. Ted Harkins and knew that the medication he found to help Pete helped him to be able to work even if it was part-time and to have contact with his family, even if it was only on the weekends. He would be ever so grateful to Ted Harkins for his tremendous contribution in his life.

Slowly Pete began to react to the people around him in a more positive manner. It wasn't long before Pete Gallagher began to develop a winning smile and a tremendous zest for life – much more like the "old" Pete. He still had lots of hurdles to overcome, but Pete was becoming more and more accepting of the life he now had. He tried hard every day to understand that all these things happened to him for a reason – someday Pete would come to understand that reason.

Pete continued to live at the Institute, working part-time a few hours a day Monday through Friday and spending his weekends at home when a family member could plan to be home with him. No one was ready to let Pete be alone – not yet – maybe never. He still needed so much attention.

With all the wonderful things coming to pass for Pete Gallagher, he just could not settle himself down to one thing for any period of time. He moved from one job to another over the next several years, never staying with one for very long. He would get frustrated with one thing or another and request to be moved again and again. Pete still had a lot of difficulty understanding other people's roles in life and felt they should be helping him do his job. As much as Pete had developed his new self, there were situations, particularly at work, where people and tasks just frustrated him and his temper and shortcomings would come out. He had difficulties understanding the people he worked with predominantly the other employees on any job site who were mentally retarded. Pete knew he was not mentally retarded but many people saw him that way. This was another obstacle that was a real difficult hurdle for Pete to climb over. It would take Pete years and years to understand how he fit into such surroundings and how his life could function when he was subjected to being stereotyped as retarded. All he wanted was to be normal again. Why couldn't he just be normal?

"I do think that Pete is responding to the medication and therapy better than he has in the past," said Dr. Faulkner. If this continues, I think he may be able to be released shortly.

"That is great news, Dr. Faulkner," said Ellie. How soon before we can take Pete home?"

"Maybe a few more months, but I'm sure it will be soon," responded Dr. Harkins.

"That is wonderful news," said Ellie. "I'm sure all the family will be so excited to have Pete home again."

Pete spent the next several months at the Institute getting all sorts of treatment, from an assortment of medication to tremendous amounts of psychological counseling. After some time, family and medical professions began to see enough improvement to send Pete home.

The day finally arrived when Pete was released to go home – home to live a "normal" life again with his parents.

His family was so exuberant that Dan Gallagher decided to take his family on a cross-county vacation and celebrate being together again. Jane had so many other commitments now, she was in college so she opted to stay at home that summer and continue her studies and other obligations. Dan Gallagher rented a motor home and loaded his boys and wife for a fabulous vacation – one that Pete would remember for the rest of his life.

It was a great time and Pete was wonderful – no acting out, no outburst and although the doctors warned he might experience seizures, none happened. This was truly what they had all hoped for.

Pete had to be careful as walking was still an ordeal, but he managed with lots of help. Pete had been left with partial paralyzation on his left side, using his arm, his hand, his left leg and foot were very difficult. Pete had a real tough time with his left foot not wanting to stay on the ground, but that wasn't going to ruin his trip. He was still learning how to use his arm and hand from the shoulder down. He was determined he would adapt over time. He was determined that this vacation would be a good time and it was for everyone.

Once back home after their month-long vacation, Dan and Ellie were comfortable getting Pete prepared to go back to high school and finish his senior year.

Dan and Ellie made all the provisions for Pete to return to his high school and pick up his studies where he had left off the year before. He would now enter his senior year of high school and both Dan and Ellie prayed that Pete would be able to finish his high school studies and go on to college as they had planned before his accident.

"Dan, I think we need to get clothes for Pete before school starts," said Ellie. He has changed in size a great deal since being in the hospital. He has lost the bulky statute, but I think he has grown an inch."

"That sounds like a great plan," replied Dan. "Why don't you take him and get him the things he needs before the weekend and then he can show them off to me on Saturday. He'll want new athletic shoes and that may be a problem."

"I'll do what I can and we'll get him some clothes and work on the shoes later if necessary," responded Ellie.

Pete began his senior year with eager anticipation, yet inside Pete was anxious about all the things that the future would bring. His peers saw him now as defective and different. They looked at him as though he was from outer space. Just how was he going to live with the social stigma that his brain injury had caused? If that wasn't enough, could he remember the things he was taught long enough to pass any given subject?

It wasn't long, however, when Pete's paranoia set in -- in full force. Pete thought that people from everywhere were out to get him. His teachers were against him because he couldn't remember. His classmates were against him and had it out for him because he messed up at a football game – that must be why everyone was following him.

"Hey, Joe," accused Pete. "I know you followed me to the drug store last night. Why did you do that? I don't need you following me around."

"I didn't follow you Pete," said Joe.

"Yeah, you did and I want you to stop it right now!" said Pete as he pushed Joe against the wall.

"Man, I don't know what your problem is, but I didn't nor do I desire to follow you anywhere," exclaimed Joe. "I have better things to do." Joe moved out of Pete's swing and ran out of sight before Pete could utter anything further.

Pete thought one person after another was following him and he felt the presence of other people behind him all the time. He accused everyone who tried to befriend him or to get near him of following him and trying to hurt him. Pete moved slowly and he thought everyone around him were angry with him because he was in their way. One day Pete took a swing at the maple tree standing on the front lawn of his school. He broke his hand and went into a fit of rage against the tree. School officials came to try to help Pete but he was like a frightened tiger and wouldn't let anyone touch him. There was nothing left to do but to get Pete the help he needed and to get him protected from himself. Pete landed back in the Institute where he would spend the next four years of his life trying to deal with the rest of the world and how it related to him.

Pete would have to learn what others expected of him, their ideas about life, and how to become an important part of society and live independently. Life was to take on another new meaning for young Pete. The hardest lessons were yet to be learned by this now almost eighteen-year old brain-injured paranoid Pete Gallagher.

Now back at the Institute, Pete had more of the same difficulties – trying to accept who he was. If Pete's life was not complicated enough, he found as much trouble as he could muster living at the Institute and trying to make friends with other troubled young people. He seemed attracted to all the wrong friends at the Institute. If they could manage to find the wrong things to do, Pete was right there.

One such instance got Pete caught climbing over a fence on property clearly marked 'no trespassing'. Pete's left side couldn't keep up with his body and thus Pete spent months in a cast to mend his broken leg and ankle. He just wanted to be like the other guys – he wanted all of him to function properly. He had lots of difficulty understanding why that was just not happening.

Pete also was a normal young male and sought the affections of the opposite sex as much as possible. If he saw a young lady who might give him a moment of attention, Pete felt he was in love. This part of his development was a confusing event for him as well as having to learn how to treat and be around the 'ladies'.

Dan Gallagher found himself in the position of having to constantly remind Pete of his shortcomings.

"Pete, you just should not be thinking about marriage and a family. You are never going to get married and have a family. You just need to get that into your head," said Dan Gallagher to his emotional son.

"Yes, I am. I don't see why I can't have a wife and live just like you and mom," interjected Pete.

"You have limitation, Pete. You just need to get these thoughts out of your head."

"I don't want to get them out of my head. The ladies are fine people and I like them. I want to fall in love with someone and have her love me back. That's all I want."

"Pete, that's enough. Stop this talking about marriage, a wife and family – it's just not going to happen, that's all, it's just not going to happen. You just need to be grateful that you are alive and learn to be happy with what you have. That's it – this conversation is over."

How Dan Gallagher could explain to his son that he would never be able to have employment to fully support himself, much less a wife and children or a house and all those responsibilities. How could he explain to his son that he would never be able to do the things that are required of a husband and a father? No, he decided he would not try to explain these things to Pete – he would just not understand – there was no explaining this to Pete.

Pete Gallagher was trying to learn how to deal with life – a life that was very new and different. This new life, however, had too many rules and regulations. All that Pete wanted was to have a wife, a family, and live his life in much the same way as his parents and their friends had. Pete still had a hard time understanding why his life needed to be so different. He just wanted what every other young man wanted – didn't he? Would he ever be able to have his dream?

Chapter VII

Nanette's Rough Marriage to Sam

Jake and Nanette spent a few extra days in the hospital after Jake's birth to make sure that Nanette would be able to function at home. Nanette had gone through a horrible birth process having Jake. Three days after his birth, Nanette felt great and got out of bed and headed to the bathroom on her own. When she exited the bathroom, she saw Jake in his bassinette, made a noise, and fell to the floor. Jake sensed his mother's problems and cried at the top of his lungs. That little exercise kept Nanette and Jake in the hospital an extra day.

Sam brought Jake and Nanette home from the hospital, however, since Sam had to return to Boston to finish the family room for Erica, Nanette decided to spend some time with her parents to get Jake's new life going the way it should. Sam stayed with them at her parents for the weekend, returning to Boston on Monday morning.

Nanette's rough delivery took a toll on her. She had difficulty sitting or standing for any length of time, but she attended to her new baby the way a first-time mother who had fallen in love with her son.

"He is so beautiful," said Ann Peters, Nanette's mother

"He sure is, how did I get so lucky? If I could just make Jake stop crying so much, then you and dad might get some rest too. He just doesn't seem to settle down," responded Nanette.

"Don't you worry about us, honey. You just take care of your baby. I think he has a lot of gas. Perhaps some peppermint in his formula might help him to get it passed."

"I'll try that. Thanks, mom."

The next couple of weeks were difficult as Nanette attempted to get Jake's gassy tummy settled. It was finally determined he was allergic to milk and was put on soymilk to help him. That seemed to do the trick but Sam thought she was coddling little Jake too much. Nanette was so frustrated. This was a tiny two week old who baby who needed coddling and his mother's nurturing. Her precious little son would have it no matter what Sam said!

Nanette never heard much from Sam, but he would call every few days.

"You're going to make a mama's boy out him," Sam yelled.

"He's just a tiny baby trying to get started in life," Nanette responded.

"Yeah and he's got you wrapped around his little finger."

The arguments continued over how to care for little Jake. Day in and day out Sam and Nanette fought about how to take care of their son mostly over the phone. Sam continued to stay in Boston and told Nanette that the family room was taking longer than expected. On one weekend when Sam finally decided to come visit his wife and son, Ann decided enough was enough.

"Sam, you and Nanette need to take Jake home next weekend. It will be Thanksgiving and I need my house to get ready for the holiday and Nanette needs to get Jake settled in his own home," Ann said in a very firm and deliberate manner.

"Okay, Ann. I'll move them home. I should be able to get the family room finished by next weekend and then I'll move them home."

"Never mind about should – that's the way it will be. You'd better plan on moving your family home next weekend."

Ann Peters was a strong and powerful woman, very determined in her own opinions but with an immense heart of gold. She was very generous, but never wanted people to take advantage of her. Sam knew that if Ann told her to get his family home, that he'd better make sure and get it done when she said. She was not a woman to be reckoned with.

Although Ann and Lee had Nanette, Sam and Jake for Thanksgiving dinner, Nanette, Sam and Jake were moved back to their own home to spend their first holiday in their own rented farmhouse.

Little Jake enjoyed his new surroundings and was surviving well until Nanette began to have more and more difficulties getting Sam to give her enough money to buy the necessary items for even his own son. Nanette had trouble coming up with eleven cents which was the cost of a jar of baby fruit the time. Would their precious son just be hungry all the time?

"Sam, I put some money in Jake's piggy bank yesterday from Aunt Gracie. I noticed it is gone. Did you take it," commented Nanette.

"Yeah, what's it to ya? I needed some beer," responded Sam

"Beer? When your son doesn't have fruit or formula to last more than a day? How could you do that Sam?"

"Easy, I needed some beer. You got a problem with that?"

"Yeah, I do. Jake needs to eat. It's one thing if I don't, but Jake needs to eat."

"Too bad. Call your mother or your Aunt Gracie. They'll give you money for Jake. They always do."

"That's not right, Sam. We shouldn't be depending on them for what Jake needs."

Sam and Nanette continued to have fights over money every day. There never was enough money for groceries or for the things little Jake needed. Nanette found herself without even toilet paper and would use whatever telephone book she could do without.

Every other day Aunt Gracie came by with a bag of things for Nanette and Jake but no longer left cash. She knew that Sam would just go buy more beer. Jimmy also stopped by with bags of groceries that Ann Peters had prepared and sent over to help Nanette and Jake. There was little concern for Sam any longer in the Peters family. He had neglected his family so much.

Sam was gone most days and long into the nights, day after day. Nanette was left with her little Jake on this 200-acre farm without a working car. Sam told Nanette that his car needed repairs and would be out of commission for the time being while they searched for the right parts. Then there was a knock on the door one sunny afternoon.

"We're looking for Sam Sullivan. Is he home?" one of two men dressed in dark suits asked Nanette as she greeted them at her screened back door.

"No, he's off working. He's not home right now," responded Nanette.

"Where is he then?"

"I don't know. He's a carpenter and is on a job right now. I think he may still be working in Boston, but I'm not sure." Nanette was beginning to be frightened now.

"Well, you tell him that if he ever wants to see his car again, he'd better show up with the money he owes us."

With that the men left and now Nanette knew the car was not just in a shop to be fixed. She would never fully know what had happened to the car, but she knew her husband owed these men money – either money for the car or they were holding his car for a gambling debt, something she had worried about.

Things were getting worse by the day and Nanette knew that she and her son were facing some serious problems if something wasn't done soon.

"Where's the checkbook?" yelled Sam as he stormed in the house one early Friday afternoon in January.

"It's in your desk but there's no money in the account. What are you doing, Sam?" replied Nanette.

"My driver's license has to be renewed and so does the registration on my car. I just got pulled over by a cop and my license is expired. I have to go get it renewed like today."

"We don't have enough money anywhere. You'll have to ask your sister or brother-in-law for the money."

"No, you call your folks and ask them."

"No, I won't. They help us every day with food and groceries. I'm not going to them for more money. You ask your family this time. This is your need anyway."

"Look, witch. Call your folks and get the money. I have to go see some men and if I don't have that money by the time I return in an hour, you'll suffer some serious consequences," demanded Sam.

Nanette was so scared. She was very afraid of what Sam had gotten into. She was afraid of what he was going to do. She needed to know where to turn. She called her mother.

"Mom, Sam is off on a tangent again. I don't know what he is capable of. He wants me to come up with money for his license and registration in the next hour or he said I would suffer serious consequences. What am I going to do?"

"Hang up from me and call Attorney Cory Patrelli who you used to work for before Jake was born. He'll know what to do. I'm going to call Aunt Gracie right now.

"Okay, mom. I'll call Attorney Patrelli now.

Nanette hung up and made the call to Attorney Patrelli explaining her entire situation to him over the phone.

"Nanette, you have to liquidate everything you have. It sounds to me like Sam already has gotten into some financial difficulties. Maybe some of these troubles could be illegal activities that could put you and your baby in harm's way. Get yourself and your baby out of there immediately. Tomorrow morning, I want you to come see me at my office," Attorney Patrelli advised Nanette.

Nanette returned the call to her mom who had already made plans with Aunt Gracie to come pick up little Jake and her removing them from the house. This would not be easy as there was over a foot of snow all around Nanette's rented house and half-mile long driveway, which Sam had never had plowed. Instead he used Nanette's Impala to plow it and dropped the transmission, leaving her car at the base of driveway.

Aunt Gracie and Ann Peters pulled up in front of the house on the road and climbed the large hill in snow up to their knees to the back door of the farmhouse. Nanette had loaded Jake's things and her own in laundry baskets and they moved out very quickly. They left long before Sam returned home. It was a very emotional and stressful day for Nanette, her mom and her Aunt Gracie. She'd made a break – hopefully a good break.

Nanette felt a huge burden lifted from her shoulders, however, she was very frightened as to how Sam would view her having picked up the baby and moved out. She spent the next several hours in deep conversation with her mother and aunt through lots and lots of tears. Nanette wanted her marriage to Sam to work but she was at a loss for how it was going to happen since Sam did not stay home long enough to try to communicate with her. He never allowed her to know what was going on in their finances or any other part of their lives. It was as though Sam and Nanette shared a rented house together but each with their own agenda.

Soon after supper that evening the telephone rang.

"Nanette, the phone is for you," said Ann

"Don't get too upset, honey if that is Sam. Stay strong," said Lee Peters who was a man of very few words.

"Hello," replied Nanette

"Nanette, what's happened? Why are you there?" responded Sam

"I'm not coming back, Sam. I just don't know what you're about. I don't understand why we don't have any money, why you keep your desk drawers locked, or why you don't seem to be bringing home an income, yet you go out every day, or why we don't talk. I just can't live that way anymore."

"Please, Nanette. Don't leave me. Would you go to a marriage counselor? Please don't leave me. I'll make the appointment, but please would you just go to a marriage counselor with me."

"Are you sure, Sam? Are you sure you want to try to make this marriage and our lives work?"

"Oh, yes, Nanette, yes. Please, please go with me to a marriage counselor."

"All right. You make the arrangements and I'll go with you."

Lee and Ann Peters looked at each other as their daughter spoke to her husband on the phone. They heard the conversation but wasn't sure their daughter was making the right choices. On the other hand, it was not their lives and they had to let her live her life the way she felt necessary.

Nanette and Sam started marriage counseling two days later with a Catholic Priest. Nanette felt there might be hope since Sam seemed to open up to the counselor better than he had with her in all the years they had been together. This was the first time in her life Nanette felt in control of what might happen to her and Sam. Sam was beginning to really make sense, and she was hopeful that things just might turn around.

As promised, the day after Nanette moved out of their home, she went to visit her former employer, Attorney Cory Patrelli. He talked to her in a voice she never heard before – stern, yet promising. He told her what she needed to do to protect herself and then he said something to her that would remain with her for the rest of her life.

"Little lady, you need to grow up and you need to begin to do that right now, right here, with me," shouted Cory Patrelli. "I want you to come back to work for me. You need a job and I need some help around here that can understand my needs. What do you say?"

In a very stunned voice, Nanette responded, "But I have a small baby. Yes, I need the work but I can't work full time with a three-month old baby."

"Then part-time. You name it. When can you work"

"Okay. How about three days a week from 9:00 a.m. to 3:00 p.m."

"Fine - can you start tomorrow?"

"No, I will start on Monday. I will have to make arrangements for Jake. I'm sure my mother will watch him, but I need to make sure."

Nanette now had a part-time job for three days a week. That lasted only one week and was soon turned into four days a week. She didn't mind working later but kept Wednesdays for Jake, to spend some time with her fast-growing son. Those were precious days for her and she was not about to give up that time with Jake.

At end of January, however, with the help of her father and brother, Nanette moved everything out of the rented farmhouse. During that move, Sam became very drunk and began throwing things out of windows. His close friend had to get him out of the house and away so that Nanette could do what needed to be done -- liquidate their liabilities and try for a new beginning.

Sam called Nanette at her parents' home that very evening begging for a chance to make their marriage work. Sam asked Nanette if she would agree to marriage counseling if he could get something set up. Nanette agreed not wanting to make every effort to save her marriage and the commitment she had made on her wedding day. They met weekly with a catholic priest who specialized in marriage counseling. They seemed to be making progress or at least Nanette thought they were.

The next five months were not the easy on either family. Living back home with an influencing mother and father took a toll on Nanette. She wasn't sure any more whether she was making her own decisions or was she falling back on what her parents told her what she should do.

After five long months of counseling and much to her parents' disapproval, Nanette agreed to get an apartment and move back with Sam. She and Sam found a small apartment but big enough for them and Jake in the back of a post office in the neighboring town. There was two bedrooms so Jake could have his own room and a comfortable enough place although small.

There was a lot of tension between Lee and Ann Peters and Nanette and Sam Sullivan during this time when Nanette and Sam were so desperately trying to make their marriage work. Nanette had to step back and remove herself from her family long enough to attempt a life with Sam -- that's what her marriage vows had said and she was determined to make them work. That was what her parents had instilled in her and yet they didn't see her side of the situation at all. She felt strongly that since she made a commitment to Sam, she was going to do whatever it took to make good on that commitment.

Nanette and Sam worked hard on trying to make their marriage work. The next few months over the beautiful summer months were some of the best moments they had shared. Having Jake was everything to the both of them. He was such a sweet boy and they both enjoy spending as much time with him as they could. They continued, however, to be on a strict financial budget that seemed to upset Sam very much.

"Please wake up, Nanette", Sam pleaded. I need my $3.00 for today so I can buy my coffee and smokes.

"Ok, bring me my purse, please," squeaked Nanette in her sleepy voice. She didn't need to get up at 6:00 a.m. except to give Sam his daily allowance. This was the only way she could keep him from spending on things like beer or gambling.

Then one day Sam came home with news.

"I am getting a used television from my boss at the apartment management company. I think it was left over from a tenant who moved out and he said we could have it. Since we don't have one, I thought it would be great."

"Sounds good, but I don't want us to just watch television and not communicate," exclaimed Nanette. We have worked hard to make the time we have together meaningful and it is working. You love your television, some times more than me and I don't want it to become the only voices you hear again.

"It won't. It won't."

Sam brought the television home the end of that week and by Sunday Nanette saw Sam more glued to the screen than ever. He hardly spoke two words to her that entire weekend. The television did exactly what she had hoped it would not do - pull Sam away from her again.

Nanette had now begun to work four days a week at the law firm with Wednesdays off. She was still only part-time spending as much time as she could with Jake. She knew, however, that Sam's income would not be enough to keep them on their strict budget. She was very frugal saving money on groceries wherever she could and using that savings to buy Jake a new undershirt or a pair of socks. She enjoyed every afternoon with him and she and Jake spent every dinner time together. Sam didn't get home until 6:30 most evenings and Jake was ready for bed by the time Sam arrived.

This apartment had no bathtub so for a little while it was okay to bath Jake in the sink but soon he became too big to do that anymore. So Nanette had carefully used a baby bathtub in the bottom of the shower to give Jake a bath before his dad got home. He would be all fed, bathed and smelling wonderful by the time Sam got home from a very long day at work.

Arriving home his usual time, Sam pushed himself inside the door away from Jake. "Can't you take care of this kid!" He's always climbing all over me. Take this brat and do something with him. I'm too busy for this."

Sam headed straight for the refrigerator where he put the remainder of his six-pack of beer away and opened another can for himself. He plopped in his favorite chair and flipped on the television. Jake tried hard to get his daddy's attention but Sam just pushed him away, pushing him into a corner and snapping his fingers in his face. Nanette quickly grabbed Jake and brought him into his room. She sat in the rocking chair her grandmother had given her from the family farm just so she could rock Jake. She rocked and rocked little Jake until he fell sound asleep. She gently laid him in his crib as she heard Sam yelling again.

"Where is my supper. Don't you ever do anything around here. I want to eat and I want to eat now!"

"I'm coming, Sam. It's all ready. I've kept it hot for you."

"Then bring it to me in the living room so I can watch TV."

"Ok, coming."

Sam didn't think it was quite fast enough and got up to see what was keeping her. Running his fingers across the wanes coating, "You need to keep this house cleaned every day. Don't you understand how to keep house? What's the matter with you?. You need to keep up."

Nanette was on the verge of tears but knew that would only make matters worse. She put Sam's dinner out for him and quickly grabbed a wet cloth and washed all the wanes coating in the kitchen and down the hall of their tiny apartment while Sam ate his dinner and watched his television.

These types of evenings were the norm for their household. Nanette put up with it hoping it would get better for Jake's sake. It didn't. It progressively got worse if anything. The days and weeks went along much the same way with Sam disturbed about something most every evening.

It was late October when Sam called to say he would be very late coming home. There had been a fire in one of the tenant houses where he was Construction Manager. There were lots of people who would be without homes that night. Nanette felt bad and told Sam not to worry that she and Jake were fine. Sam returned home about 4:00 a.m. the next morning. He wasn't drunk which surprised Nanette, but he was very different, very emotional -- a side she had not seen in him before. He told her about a four-year old little boy who had been in the fire. The boy would be okay but it just affected Sam so emotionally. He told Nanette that he wanted to enlarge their family and have another child. She was beside herself. Having another child when their marriage was no prize did not appeal to Nanette and she told Sam that. But Sam was determined and he forced himself on her. Nanette cried all night long and was determined never to go near Sam again. She woke the next morning ashamed and full of black and blues. Sam never mentioned the night before or how she looked. He just went about his usual business of getting ready to return to work. Nanette would never be the same again.

Nanette and Sam became more and more distant as the days moved on into weeks. Nanette continued to work part-time four days a week getting Jake up early every day to do the chores before work. She would get the laundry started in their own washer and take the wet clothes to the laundromat to put it in the dryer. It meant taking Jake out of the car and putting his now car seat onto the stroller wheels to push him and the laundry into the laundromat. Then the repeat to put Jake back in the car and Nanette would take him off to the babysitter. During her lunch hour she drove back to the laundromat to fold the dried clothes. Nanette's hours were jammed packed with things to do.

Jake began to develop allergies and his doctor told Nanette that she needed to wet mop all the flooring in the apartment every day. So Nanette began a new chore every morning. She would put Jake in his car seat in the car just outside the apartment. She left the door open and would wet mop all the floors on her way out the door. One more thing she needed to remember to do.

"Where is my son," Sam yelled as he came through the door – like most nights. His coming home was later and later these days.

"He's in bed, Sam. It's past 7:30 p.m. and you know Jake goes to sleep at 7:00 p.m.

"I want to see my son." Sam walked into the sleeping baby's room. He picked Jake up and stood him on the floor.

Jake was still half asleep and wobbled to and fro as he tried to balance himself. He was only barley a year old and very new at walking. Sam thought this was funny to see Jake wobble around in a daze. Before long Jake began to understand he was being made to wake up and started to cry.

"Shut that brat up or I'll shut him up but good," Sam bellowed.

Nanette knew he meant it too. He had become in the habit of doing this to little Jake and it upset her so much. She grabbed Jake and held him close until he stopped crying. All too often when Sam woke Jake, Nanette had a difficult time getting the child back to sleep. In order to prevent Sam from beating the precious baby, Nanette would stay up with Jake all night and rock him in her rocking chair. Jake would sleep peacefully on her shoulder and if she was lucky enough, she just might get a little sleep herself while holding her baby as close and tight as she could.

The days began to get cooler and cooler as the beautiful fall leaves began to change color. The crispness of the air was so refreshing and the smells of hot apple and pumpkin pie were beginning to wave through the air around the neighborhood. Thanksgiving was only a few days away now. Sam, Nanette and Jake were planning on spending the holiday and long weekend with Sam's sister and family and their dad in Boston. It would be a great trip, but Nanette was concerned because now she would be forced to be near Sam again, something she had not done since that horrible night in September. She had kept that a secret to everyone and denied a lot of her own feelings about that evening. Now she was faced to have to deal with Sam on an intimate level again. For the sake of the family, she would once again do what she had to do and keep her mouth shut.

Nanette had been assisting in the choir of the church that Attorney Petrelli's wife, Mary attended. One Sunday morning in September before

Nanette even suspected she was pregnant but after Sam had forced himself on her, Nanette was rehearsing with the choir before church. When rehearsal was over, Nanette bent down to pick up her music materials. Nanette felt a man's hand on her back, and a deep voice who said, "So you're going to have another baby, huh!" Thinking it was one of the other choir members, she looked up to respond, but no one was there. They had all gone to dress in choir gowns and have a cup of coffee. As frightening as this experience was, Nanette knew she had just felt God's presence. Did this conversation with God mean what she thought it meant?

Only a couple of weeks after the holiday, Nanette began to have signs of morning sickness and she knew in her heart that she was pregnant again. She was in for a ride of her life over the next months ahead. How would she ever explain any of this to her parents? She wouldn't, she couldn't -- she didn't dare! They already hated Sam for taking her away again.

"Sam, I have an appointment to see the doctor tomorrow and I'd like you to come with me," said Nanette one evening when Sam returned from work.

"What do you need me for? You seem to have everything in order. Go by yourself. I can't be running around to hold your hand."

Nanette felt Sam's rejection again and felt worse than ever. She went to her appointment alone and although she was convinced she was pregnant, the doctor told her she was not. He said she would probably begin her period any time now but that she was not pregnant. Nanette tried to be relieved but after having one child she knew she was going to have another. She had a second test and a third test done in the doctor's office within the next month and a half but still the doctor said she was not pregnant. Finally the fourth test confirmed that she was indeed pregnant and that she would have a baby the following August. Only two weeks later, Nanette began to show signs of losing her baby. The doctor confirmed that she would miscarry this child. Nanette had a strong feeling that she was meant to have this child.

After her previous experience at the church, she knew in her heart that God meant for her to survive this pregnancy. She knew that no matter what the doctors said, she was going to have another baby. There had to be a reason why God meant for her to have this child.

Nanette stopped one evening after work with baby Jake to visit with her parents and have some dinner. Sam was working late and would eat later. About the time they were going to leave, Nanette told them of her pregnancy but not how it happened. They were both furious and blamed Nanette for allowing this to happen.

She continued to carry her child without a miscarriage. Only a month later at the beginning of her fifth month, Nanette began to suffer back pain so severe she had a hard time taking care of Jake.

She and Sam were visiting with her parents when her back began to really give her a lot of trouble.

"What's your problem now," said Sam in a manner of disgust.

"My back is very painful," answered Nanette

"You've got something wrong with you all the time. You're just a walking nightmare."

"I can't take care of Jake the way I need to, Sam. I'm going to stay overnight with mom and dad. Mom will help me with Jake and see if I can get this back to feel better."

"Do whatever you want. You will anyway."

As was the usual case, Sam made Nanette feel guilty for trying to take care of herself and their small child. Now, however, she had to let that guilt just be a matter of no concern -- she had an unborn child to think of also. She knew she needed more assistance than Sam could ever be and thus she made the decision to stay with her parents to Sam's utter irritation. Nanette was more confused now than ever. She didn't know how she and Sam would ever live a life even close to the relationship she had witnessed between her parents all of her life. This was going to be no picnic!

Chapter VIII

Pete's Life on the Outside

Pete was now left with lots of negative thoughts. He was now in his 20's having spent years at the Institute and was living back with his parents. Confusion was the main focus of Pete's day almost every day. He was confused about how he was supposed to interact with his family – just what did they expect of him.

He was confused about what he was supposed to do at his part-time job – he now had had five different employers. Pete never remained happy at any job, constantly complaining about his bosses, his fellow employees and his own job. Pete just couldn't remember from day to day what he was supposed to do. Wasn't his boss supposed to tell him every day what he should do? Wasn't that the role of a boss?

If these things weren't enough, who were his friends supposed to be? Most of the people around him were mentally retarded. Pete had a lot of difficulty understanding his new friends and they certainly did not understand him.

One of Pete's fellow patients at the hospital stayed in touch with him after Pete was discharged. Noshua was not a good influence on Pete, however. He came from a very different home life and had been left to fend for himself during his time in the Institute.

Noshua called Pete one evening. "Hey, Pete. What are you up to these days?"

"Not much, just going to work every day and doing my job. Then I just hang out with my folks."

"Meet me tomorrow night at Dillian's Groceries at 7:00 p.m. okay?"

"Yeah, okay, see you then."

Pete had been introduced back to driving and had taken the car out now and then but mostly with supervision. His favorite car – the Mustang he so proudly had restored to a personal expression of himself – the car that was supposed to be his graduation present -- had now been totaled by his younger brother, Stan. However, if he played his cards right, stayed out of trouble over the next day or so, perhaps his dad would let him take the family car. Then again, Pete was afraid to ask his father because he always had a reason why he shouldn't do something that Pete wanted to do.

The next morning was Saturday and Pete knew that his father would be off to play golf with his buddies and be gone a good portion of the day. Once he was gone, Pete decided he might be better if he approached his mother about using her car.

Ellie was in the kitchen cleaning and preparing things for dinner for Saturday night and a few things ahead so she could relax more on Sunday after church. Sundays were a family day, but she always prepared a nice Sunday dinner. If she made some of the cold items and placed pickles and relishes in trays, she could have an easier time of finishing the dinner after church. Jane was now such a big help when she was home, but now that Pete was back home again, he too helped get things ready. How she loved having the family together for mealtimes. She always took out her fine china and sterling silver for Sunday dinner. So all the special serving pieces came out then as well. She was a firm believer, as was her mother, that the family should get used to using and enjoying the finer things in life and so the special dishes and silver came out every Sunday.

"Mom, I need to talk to you about something," said Pete.

"What is it, Pete?" inquired Ellie

"A few of my friends are meeting up tonight at the ice cream parlor in town," Pete lied about how many of his friends would be there and where they were meeting. He knew his parents didn't approve of Noshua and it might be better if he just didn't tell them who or where he was meeting his friends. He wasn't a child anymore and he just needed to use the car. "Would it be okay if I took your car to meet them?"

"Well, Pete, your father is off playing golf right now. We'll have to wait until he comes home and ask him," said Ellie.

"Oh, mom, please. You know, dad. He always finds a reason why I can't take the car out by myself. Please, mom, just let me take your car," cried Pete.

"That's not true, Pete. Your father just wants the best for you."

"Yeah, he just wants to treat me like a baby and keep me locked up for life just because I had a brain injury," replied Pete in utter disgust. I'm not a freak but the way dad acts, you'd think I was the biggest freak of the world!"

"Now, Pete, you know that's not true."

"Yeah, well tell me the last time he ever let me just drive a car alone to meet my friends."

Ellie Gallagher knew Pete was right and her heartstrings had been pulled by one of her children again! If she let Pete use the car, her husband was sure to get upset. However, if she didn't, she also knew she was holding Pete back from maturing into a grown man. After all whether any of them liked it or not Pete would become a man. If her husband kept denying Pete the chance to prove himself, make his own mistakes in life, then Pete would always be dependent upon some other person, even if they were gone. Ellie thought and thought about how she should respond to her son and if she was making the right decision if she did allow him to use her car. She realized she would have to take the heat if her husband got upset -- so be it. She had to give Pete a chance.

"Okay, Pete. You can take my car but you must be home by 10:00 p.m. – not one minute later or you'll have a huge price to pay."

"Thanks, mom," exclaimed Pete in enthusiastic excitement. "I knew you'd understand. Thanks, really thanks! I'll be home by 10:00 p.m. -- promise!"

Pete was so excited. He was now going to have the independence he had craved for so long. He was going to take the car out all by himself and meet his friends – or rather he was going to meet up with Noshua.

Saturday night came and Pete took his shower, shaved well, and put on some jeans and a new shirt. He wasn't sure what Noshua had in mind and if they met up with some young ladies, that would be okay too. Their rendezvous plans happened as scheduled.

Pete quietly walked down the stairs in the hopes of not running into his father. He was somewhere but not in clear sight, so Pete just grabbed his mom's car keys and quietly crept out the back door and into the garage. He held his breath as he moved slowly and quietly. Once the garage door opened, Pete was quick to start the engine and move quickly out of the driveway. Out on the open road, he began to breathe easy again. He was safe from the scrutiny of his father and the use of his mother's car -- the family car.

Pete was careful to obey all the rules of the road. It sure wouldn't do any good to get caught by a policeman and get a ticket. That would not help his case with his dad about having some independence via the use of the family car.

As Pete approached Dillian's grocery store, he saw Noshua in his car parked off to the right in the large lot.

"Hey, Noshua, how's it going," said Pete. "Good to see you. What you been up to? It's been a long time since I saw you last; what about three months now?"

"Yeah, something like that. Hey look what I have," Noshua pointed to a case of beer in the back of his car.

"How did you get that!" exclaimed Pete

"Don't ask. Just enjoy!"

The two young men drank, and talked in Noshua's car for hours. Once fully intoxicated the two young men made a scheme to head down to the local package store and get some more, by force as Noshua said was necessary since neither had enough money. Noshua planned they would just park his car in the woods behind the store, hop the fence, focus themselves on the owner making him believe they had a gun, and grab what they wanted. They'd be off and out of sight before any police could ever get there.

Pete so craved the attention of someone and the idea of doing something that he knew was wrong just to prove to himself that he could do it and get away with it. It sounded like just a rush and one he was willing to do. Pete was just running on adrenaline and wasn't making much sense of this stupid plan of Noshua's.

Everything went according to plan until they tried to "hop" the fence as Noshua had claimed. Not such an easy task for Pete. His left side just would not cooperate. His partially paralyzed leg always got in the way and it just would not hop over the fence the way Noshua had. He fell hard on his right side and both of the young men heard Pete's leg give a huge snap as he landed. Now in horrific pain, neither of them were interested in completing the planned attack and now knew this had been a very stupid plan. Noshua knew he needed to get help to Pete and soon. He rushed over to the package store owner and asked him to call for some emergency help for Pete.

Both the young men were lucky they had not succeeded in fulfilling their scheme to rob the package store. Pete knew he would have to hear the wrath from his father, an unpleasant thought at best. Once in the emergency room, his parents were called.

"Pete, how many times have I told you that no good comes from hanging around guys like Noshua," yelled Dan Gallagher in the emergency room in front of all the nurses and other patients. "Furthermore, who gave you permission to take the family car anyway?"

"Mom did, that's who and besides Noshua is my friend," responded Pete in serious pain and frustration.

"Your mother didn't tell me you were going to take the car out," said Dan.

"Did you ask her?" questioned Pete gritting his teeth because of the pain.

"Why would I," replied Dan. "I had no idea she said you could use the car!"

"If you two don't mind, Mr. Gallagher, I need to get Pete into an operating room so he can have surgery on this leg," said the nurse in charge. "All this bickering is not helping the boy's pain. Can't you keep it down or wait in the waiting room? I'll be back shortly to take Pete into a surgical room for his operation."

Dan Gallagher looked like a brick had just hit him upside his head. Pete was in pain? He had a broken leg so bad that he needed surgery? Now he did feel bad. He had attacked his son while he was already suffering enough from his wild stunt.

"Pete, you are just going to have to use better judgment when you go out in the evenings with friends," said Dan Gallagher in a much more civilized tone. "I guess I have been protecting you too long. We will need to have more discussion how to best handle yourself around your peers and how to choose the correct people to be associated with. I'm sorry you're in so much pain, son."

Dan remained with his son until they took him into surgery now realizing that Pete was receiving the worse kind of punishment he could receive. Now having broken his good leg for the second time because of something foolish. Perhaps his own pain was enough punishment to finally ensure learning a good lesson. Dan worried about his son. It was hard enough raising children without having to try to make your own flesh and blood understand the difficulties of maturing when some of this was taken away because of an accident -- an accident he wished that Pete had never had to endure. Dan left his son in the hands of the medical professionals as he left the hospital and drove home.

He was now sure that Ellie would be waiting for him and this would mean a confrontation about the car. The car -- they would have to go and pick up the car. When he arrived home, sure enough, Ellie was in the kitchen making a cup of tea.

"Before you say anything, Dan, yes I did tell Pete he could take my car," said Ellie. "I thought it was time we tried trusting him and letting him make some of his own mistakes. He is never going to mature and grow into a well-adjusted adult if we don't let go just a little. We've done a lot for him, Dan, but we have to let Pete do some things on his own." Ellie looked at Dan and thought he was drained. What had happened?

"I know, Ellie, I know," said Dan. "I started to attack Pete in the hospital when I realized that the pain he is in is probably worse than any punishment I might give him. You're right, it could have been much worse. I wonder what they thought they were doing climbing over the fence. Perhaps it's better if we don't know."

"You're, right, Dan," said Ellie. "Let's be grateful that he can have his leg fixed and get out of this mess with little residue as possible. Sometimes it's not wise to dig into our children's minds too deeply."

"I'll get Stan to help me go get the car from Dillian's," responded Dan. "We'll be back shortly."

That was the end of the caper with Pete over the car with his parents and it also ended his relationship with Noshua. Pete knew it was better this way. Pete never saw Noshua again nor ever found out what happened to him. Pete would now not only face having another surgery on his good leg to mend several broken bones, he would face more months in another hospital to recover from this broken leg -- now for the second time doing a foolish stunt.

With a half body cast, Pete now had to endure another kind of pain. He was in yet another hospital, with yet more strange faces, facing more humiliation from his friends and family. Pete faced more emotional and physical challenges every day trying hard not to let anyone know just much he was hurting inside. He wallowed in emotional upheaval daily until one day he knew he would break.

Pete's depression over his life continued day in and day out. He wondered what would ever happen to him. He wondered why he got up every morning. He became very depressed about his 'new' broken leg. He had been stupid to get drunk with Noshua and he had thought Noshua's idea to rob the liquor store was really dumb.

Pete began to think about all the stuff he heard his brothers and sister talk about what they did on the weekends. He didn't have the kind of friends who would enjoy doing any of the stuff they did. He was a loser in his mind. He didn't think he would ever figure out who he was, where he belonged, who he should hang out with or who he should believe. He wanted more than anything to just be normal. He was having a hard time understanding that normal for him was not the same normal as it was for other people.

He was different. He had short-term memory issues. He couldn't remember things from moment to moment much less a day later. His friends didn't want to hang around someone like that. He also had parts of his body that didn't work right and that made him look like a cripple. He didn't feel like a cripple. But Pete knew he looked like that to his 'old' friends and that made them feel creepy, so they didn't want to be associated with him, as though it would rub off on them. What were they thinking? He didn't have a disease -- then again maybe he did -- a disease of being a freak, a nothing. Pete lunged further and further into depression.

The days and weeks went along with Pete receiving the medical attention he needed, the physiological treatments the doctors prescribed, but inside Pete had a turmoil going on that no one knew about. He couldn't express this to any one because he himself couldn't understand what was happening. Pete was a "man" inside a *sixteen-year old body* of a young boy. Parts of him were that of a "man" and other parts of him were a *sixteen-year old boy*. It would take years and years before Pete would ever come to understand these things and a very special person in his life to help him understand himself and to learn to live with these taunting emotions.

After two months in this hospital and his leg finally mended, Pete returned to his parents' home again. He began his working career again, if one could call it that. Pete continued his treatments with all of his doctors but primarily with Ted Harkins who would continue to give Pete the help he needed for many years to come.

Dr. Harkins knew things needed to change for Pete. He couldn't continue to live with his parents, attempt to hold employment, and have the social skills that Pete was living with. Something had to change if Pete would ever have any chance for a happy life.

Soon after his release from his broken leg, Pete met a young woman while attending a session in Dr. Harkins' office. She was another patient and Pete struck up a conversation with her in the waiting room. For Pete, this was much more than just a conversation – he just knew he was in love with Shirley Laughlin.

"Would you like to go to the movies on Saturday night," asked Pete.

"Sure. That would be great, Pete," replied Shirley.

"I'll pick you up at 6:00 p.m. Just write your number and address here for me." Pete put the paper in his calendar which he kept in his pocket at all times so he wouldn't forget what to do from day to day.

Shirley and Pete began a relationship that would last for more than a year. Pete called Shirley every day and saw her at least twice a week. They talked a lot but the focus of their relationship became very sexual for Pete. He liked being around Shirley. She was an okay person and someone who would listen to him, some times. Most of the time, however, Shirley had lots of her own issues and she found it necessary to burden Pete with her problems.

Pete was still struggling with his own issues but being the kind of person he was, did not want to hurt Shirley's feelings so would listen the best he could to everything she had to say. He just loved being able to go to bed with her after he listened hard to what she was telling him. It seemed that if he made love to her, then she was okay for a while and didn't seem to get so agitated. This was their relationship and it repeated itself over and over again every time they were together just about the same way. Then one evening while they were having something to eat at Shirley's parents' house their relationship moved to the next level.

"Pete, we've been seeing each other for a long time now," said Shirley one evening.

"We sure have, Shirley. Isn't it wonderful? I think, however, we should plan to get married soon. We have been doing this for a long time and we probably should get married if we are going to keep making love," said Pete.

"Yeah, you're probably right. You need to make an honest woman of me, Pete."

The next day, Pete and Shirley visited a local jewelry shop and with the small credit card that Pete's parents had given him, they bought a small diamond engagement ring for Shirley. They were both so excited and couldn't wait to tell their families. They were going to get married. They drove to Pete's parents' house to tell his parents first.

Pete was like a high school boy with excitement. He was elated that he was finally getting married and would have the wife he had always dreamed of. Soon there would be children and his life would be complete. His parents just had to be excited for him. And his father would have to eat his words. His dad thought that no woman would marry him -- well, Shirley had said yes and they were going to get married.

Pete and Shirley bounced their way through the house to the family room where Dan and Ellie were sitting.

"Mom, dad, Shirley and I are engaged," exclaimed Pete. "We're getting married. Isn't that wonderful!"

"What do you think you are doing, Pete!" his father exclaimed. This is impossible. There is no way you can get married and take on a wife. You have to give this notion of yours up right now. Young lady, you had better forget about ever getting married to my son. It just isn't going to happen."

"Dad, you don't understand. We love each other and we want to be together all the time."

"Not going to happen, Pete. It's just not going to happen!"

"But dad, you thought no woman would have me," cried Pete totally in awe of his father's reaction. "Shirley wants me for her husband and together we will be very happy and have our own little family."

"Pete, I'm telling you this is just not going to happen," shouted Dan even more agitated now than ever. "You are not going to take on a wife and the responsibilities of all that much less a family of children. Not going to happen, Pete. I won't allow it, and that's final."

Pete turned to his mother who just looked blankly at Pete and then at Shirley. Ellie knew Pete was not accepting this explanation and she wondered if he was capable of understanding what marriage and family was all about. She also knew that Dan was not giving Pete any solid reasoning that Pete might be able to understanding why marriage was not a good thing for him. Could any of them make Pete understand this? He so wanted to be normal and like the rest of his family with spouses and children. Pete had a lot of shortcomings that would never allow for this to happen. Her son would never be able to have a wife and children. How could she make him understand that?

Pete took Shirley's arm and balanced her as they walked slowly out of the house and back into the car. Once in the car they both sobbed together. They were so beside themselves and emotions were high. How could this be happening now when Pete finally had a chance for a future he so wanted.

Shirley was in a flood of tears as Pete drove her to her parents' home where she resided. They went in together to try to give them the good news, not sure it was good news any longer.

"Shirley, that's wonderful. We'll have to sit and talk about all this," said her mother.

Pete thought well at least this side of the family seemed more accepting. Little did he realize that the comment was just a patronizing one to avoid a scene, unlike at his house, in front of Pete. Shirley's parents were not any happier with the news than his and since they had already made other plans, it was really a non-issue for them and no need to upset this evening for the happy couple.

The next day, Shirley called Pete to tell him that her parents were moving to the mid-west and that she would be moving with them. Pete was devastated with the news. He thought for the first time that his dream of getting married was really going to happen in spite of his father's ranting and raving. Pete had such high hopes of having a wife and family of his own. The thought that he could not work full time and provide financially for a family of his own just never crossed his mind.

The succeeding days after this bad news, Pete began to be more and more withdrawn and put him in a deeper and deeper depression. He felt as though he just couldn't keep going on like this day after day without any hope of a normal life. He knew he was different, but somehow he just didn't want to believe it. Now with Shirley gone, his father being stronger than ever about his never having the dream of his life, Pete was slowly sinking deeper and deeper into despair.

One Sunday afternoon, Pete decided that he couldn't deal with this way of life any longer. He went to his prescription bottles and took more than a handful of these powerful drugs. Within minutes Pete began to get sleepy and laid on his bed knowing that it all would soon be over. He shut his eyes to the world he knew – to this world of reality he didn't want to know any longer. There was a beautiful white cloud in front of him and a light that shone brighter than any light he had ever seen. He felt very peaceful. Then a man in a long white robe, much like before, came from these beautiful white clouds. Before Pete could reach him, the man had him by the arm and very forcibly led him back away from the beautiful light and white cloud.

"Pete, you have a lot of work left to do and it isn't done yet," said this angel of mercy. "You must continue for there is much more ahead for you."

Pete could not understand this. He wasn't capable of doing any work. He was a nothing. He could not hold any job for long, much less work at something for years and years. What was this angel trying to tell him? Whatever kind of work could there be for Pete?

Pete did not know that he was being saved by the good Lord above for work that would prove some of the most rewarding and profound he would ever have imagined. He would help so many people to understand and appreciate life because of the trials he himself had been through. He would convey to young and old alike how well worth living life really was. He would come to know that every bit of assistance one human being can provide to another makes getting up every day with a smile worth it all. Pete also could not know now that the Lord above had a very special kind of love waiting for him and only him -- Pete Gallagher would find his happiness but he would have to work for it every day.

Pete Gallagher woke up in the hospital once again with his family all by his side. They were all so glad to know he was awake and would be okay given time. The love that poured out that day in that hospital room among every Gallagher member was a sight to behold. For the first time in young Pete's mind he began to feel as though his family not only cared for him, but that they truly did love him and did care what happened to him. It was not just the love he felt from his mother and his strong-willed father, but also the love that shone that day from each of his brothers and his older sister that made him feel such warmth. For the first time, Pete Gallagher knew that the love he felt this day from his father was stronger than he had ever known. There was a bonding that happened that day between Pete and his father that would remain with Pete Gallagher for the rest of his life – a bond no one would break and no amount of strict harsh tones would ever diminish. Pete really loved his dad and he now knew his dad loved him too!

Chapter IX

Nanette's Continued Turmoil

She was embarking on a new chapter in her life, yet emotionally Nanette was a mess. The love of her life, or so she thought, had let her down, had mistreated her, had cheated on her, and had given her delusions about raising a family - a family she so desperately wanted. How often Sam had told her that she better deliver sons to fight the battles of war because if she gave him a daughter, he would kill the baby! Now pregnant, not out of her own desire, but out of his intentional forcing, she was afraid for herself and her unborn child - a child she was now determined more than ever to have - to be a sibling to the son she already cherished!

Sam and Nanette fought about how to raise Jake, how to manage their finances, how he drank too many beers, how he stayed out so late every night, and a variety of other issues and did so in front of her parents and in their home. Sam never seemed to mind where or when he entertained a domestic encounter with his wife. Now tormented by negative memories, Nanette recalled the time when Sam became so upset about how clean she kept Jake, changing his clothes three or four times a day. Now Sam had interfered with her mothering skills again, something she was very confident about, acquiring very sufficient nurturing skills from her own mother who she deemed a great role model as a mother.

"He's your son, anyway. Keep him squeaky clean, untouchable for all I care. I'm out of here," Sam yelled at the top of his lungs. Sam walked out of her parents' home, across the driveway and never once turned around. Nanette knew at that moment he was walking out of their lives forever. She watched him walk away as their son cried out over and over for his daddy across the wooden gate that kept little Jake secured from falling down the stairs. Now the wooden gate kept him away from his own daddy -- the daddy that had become estranged and part time. Little Jake was hurt and wounded even at this young age of only fourteen months.

Nanette knew life would be different, yet she felt safe in a very protected place - the home of her parents where she grew up. She knew her father and mother would protect her from any physical harm Sam might try to impose on her.

Nanette's back was in horrible turmoil as she came downstairs the next morning. She had already called her boss to let him know she would be out for a couple of days. He was very unhappy with her and said some very insulting things to her on the phone. It didn't matter what he said. She had a son to protect and an unborn baby who both needed their mother alive and well in order to take care of them properly. She was determined to do just that no matter what it took.

Ann Peters stood over the stove stirring oatmeal when Nanette entered the kitchen. Ann knew enough about medicine to know what she saw in her daughter was not good.

"Nanette, are you okay?" said Ann.

"My back is very sore, but I feel okay. Why, Mom? You sound like I should be feeling bad. Is there something I should know?"

"You have what looks like to me, a broken blood vessel in your eye. I'm going to call Lily Reynolds and get her advice."

"Okay, if you think so."

Ann Peters made the call to Nanette's nurse friend who knew about toxemia first hand. Ann was afraid her daughter was in a more serious state than anyone expected.

Lily told Ann to call the obstetrician and that she would be right down. Lily knew the situation was probably serious and she wasted no time in getting out the door. She arrived at the Peters' house fifteen minutes later. By then, Ann had already received the word from the doctor's office to bring Nanette in right away.

"Just let me say good-bye to Jake. He's next door playing in the sand box," said Nanette anxious about her young son playing next door.

"He's having a good time. Don't interrupt him," exclaimed Lily knowing full well the seriousness of getting Nanette into the doctor and probably the hospital as soon as possible. If this was toxemia, then she knew full well that not only was Nanette's life in danger, but more importantly the life of her unborn baby.

Lily softly and calmly spoke to Nanette all the way to the doctor's office in very general conversation so as not to disturb her and to prevent her from getting anxious over the pending situation. The last thing Lily wanted to do was upset Nanette knowing that there was a strong possibility her blood pressure was already elevated and did not want to cause it to raise any further.

Twenty minutes later, Lily pulled into the doctor's office, which was adjacent to the hospital. She walked very calmly with Nanette to the door of the building where she insisted that Nanette let her push her in a wheelchair. Dr. Ronald Mallis saw Nanette within five minutes after she entered the waiting room. After only ten minutes of examing her, he asked for Lily to join them.

"Nanette, I am sending you over to the hospital right now. Can you take her Miss Reynolds?" said Dr. Mallis.

"Absolutely, doctor. I'll be happy to do so."

"Please get dressed, Nanette and I'll give Miss Reynolds all the information you will need."

Nanette proceeded to get dressed and thought she was about to have more testing done. No other thoughts entered her mind, until she emerged from the examining room and heard Lily talking to the nurses at the desk

"What do you mean, I'm being admitted? What for?" screamed Nanette.

"You have toxemia, Nanette, exclaimed Dr. Mallis. You need to be in the hospital where I can monitor you very closely or you will lose your baby. He will be stillborn. It's your choice."

Nanette was so taken back she began to cry. How could this be? She had done everything she was told, ate right, had only gained nine pounds and was in the beginning of her sixth month. She was beside herself. She had not said good-bye to Jake. What was he going to think about his mommy not coming home for dinner?

Lily very calmly put her hands on Nanette's shoulder and comforted her, telling her this was the best thing she could do for her unborn baby and for Jake who needed his little brother or sister. Lily knew that was a very important thing for Nanette – to give birth to Jake's sibling -- his very own brother or sister.

Nanette was admitted to the hospital without any pajama bottom and with a short top, no pillow, and strict instructions not to get out of bed. By the next morning and at the insistence of her doctor, Nanette was weighed and showed a loss of seven pounds overnight. It was very evident to Dr. Mallis that Nanette had to be very careful from here on out until she could deliver a healthy baby.

After five days in the hospital, Ann Peters was given a long laundry list of do's and don'ts for Nanette. Dr. Mallis told them both that they had a choice. Nanette could stay with her parents where her mother could help her with Jake, or she could hire a 24/7 live-in maid/mother's helper. Dr. Mallis explained to them the importance for Nanette to either stay "in-bed-between-sheets" or on a sofa doing absolutely nothing. He explained that any upset of any kind could make the situation much worse and harm the baby. Nanette knew that Sam and she could not afford 24/7 care for Jake and herself – that would be out of the question. Sam and she already had a very estranged relationship and she was very sure they would end in divorce. She was neither willing nor inclined to try living with Sam again. Her only alternative would be the safety net of her parents' home if they were willing to take on these responsibilities. Of course, Lee and Ann Peters had no doubt in their mind that if this is what their daughter and grandson needed, then they would do everything in their power to provide whatever they could to assist them and get the new baby born healthy no matter what it took.

Ann Peters knew that the months ahead would be difficult, that she was not young any more, and that Jake would require a lot of attention. Lee Peters would help a lot, but after all he still was working a full time job and had a part-time one as well. He was such a hard working guy and this would put a strain on them both physically and financially, but Nanette was their child and they loved these grandchildren so very dearly. Ann knew there was no option -- Nanette and her son would stay with them for however long it took to get them back on their feet.

Day in and day out, Ann Peters cooked for Nanette, keeping exactly to the very specific meal plan set out by Dr. Mallis. Nanette was not allowed off the sofa, and was given strict instructions not to lift or care for Jake in any way. Ann taught Jake how to climb chairs, to reach his dressing table, and how to bounce on his bottom to come downstairs. All these little things helped Ann Peters to care for her new extended family.

During all these months of trying hard to care for herself and Jake through the extensive help of her parents, Nanette never heard from Sam. She had tried to get some of her furniture returned from the apartment they had shared, but Sam would never communicate with her through attorneys or otherwise. The night before her baby was born, Sam delivered all of the baby things to the front porch of Ann and Lee Peters' home in the middle of the night while everyone was sound asleep. No one was aware this delivery was to be made or had been made until Lee Peter went for his morning paper.

After five months of complete bed rest, on a sunny September afternoon, Ann Peters admitted Nanette to the hospital for a scheduled cesarean section. Nanette was alone about to face going through major surgery without a husband at her side. She had begun divorce proceeding several weeks earlier and although she agreed to let Sam know when the baby was born, she was in no hurry to do so. She had given the parental rights to visit her in the hospital to Ann rather than Sam, so telling him later would be fine in Nanette's mind. She had no idea what Sam would do and she was not willing to find out any time too soon.

The following morning Nanette gave birth to a ten pound baby boy. Jamie Paul Sullivan was a normal, beautiful healthy baby boy. All of Nanette's hard work to follow the doctor's specific directions had paid off. Her new baby boy was healthy with all his fingers and toes!

Ann Peters was so relieved when Dr. Mallis called to give her the news that all the past months of toil had paid off and Nanette and Jamie would be absolutely fine. Ann knew there was still a lot of work on her for several more weeks while Nanette recovered from her operation, but she also knew the worst was behind her. She had succeeded in giving life to her new grandson and saving the life of her own daughter in the process. She sat down and cried tears of relief that both of them were okay. Lee was going to call her at noon and she would be able to give him the really good news about their newest addition to their family – Jamie Paul Sullivan.

In the weeks ahead, Ann Peters and Nanette Sullivan worked side-by-side to run their household, taking care of these two little boys they both adored and Lee Peters continued to work day and night to provide for his extended family. The three adults were all dedicated folks assuring that these two little boys would have as normal a life as possible in spite of Sam Sullivan and what he had put them all through.

The weeks moved into months and before long Jamie was crawling everywhere and Jake was getting into everything. Nanette's divorce had been put on hold as Sam had now deserted them after seeing his newest son only twice. He had deserted their apartment and possessions, leaving Nanette unable to obtain any of their furniture since the landlord held them for back rent owed. One more thing for Nanette to walk away from. Nanette sold her washer and dryer in order to buy a new dressing table for Jake that would also act as his bureau when he got older. (That one purchase stayed with Nanette for more than 30 years.)

Now with Jamie getting easier to handle, Nanette made a decision to take on a job evenings and started her own business as party demonstrator. It didn't bring home lots of money but it helped with household expenses and kept her home during the days with her two sons. Ann did what she could to help Nanette keep her business growing and still let her have time with her sons. Lee Peters needed to buy a new car and decided Nanette should have an active say in their decision, since she would need the car to make her home visits for her evening demonstrations, an act that surprised Nanette from the very beginning -- how thoughtful and kind her parents were to all of them.

Nanette, Ann and Lee Peters all worked hard to keep this little family moving forward in a positive manner. Time was flying by and before long several years had passed and Nanette and her two growing little boys were still living with Ann and Lee Peters – not that she wanted to, but she just didn't have the funds to live on her own and take care of her children.

Once Jake got into kindergarten, he began to beg his mother to attend his evening school functions. Nanette wanted to be there for Jake, but knew this would change their family structure again. Nanette gave up her business and began a full time daytime job. She was now an assistant to the General Manager of a hotel and had more responsibilities than she knew how to handle. This job meant long hours and sometimes Nanette didn't get home until almost time to put the two boys to bed. Bedtime was a precious time for her to have with her two sons, but they always ended with prayers, particularly from Jake, that God would bring them a new daddy. This broke Nanette's heart, but she vowed she would give them all she could.

Nanette was finally able to buy her own car and since the back seat could be laid down, she often took the boys on evening picnics in their pajamas. After their supper, she would lay a blanket down in the back of the car, and return home with two sleeping little boys. She did manage to attend some of Jake's school functions as she promised him she would do. Her two sons were her life and she would do whatever it took to make them happy and content children.

With Nanette's new job, Ann Peters now had even more responsibilities with the children – not the same, as everything seemed to change daily as the children grew from one stage to another. Ann was now seeing that Jake got on and off the school bus every day and was taking Jamie to nursery school three mornings a week. Life was just moving along and these children were growing and changing all the time.

It wasn't long before all this public exposure led Nanette back into the dating scene. Nanette desperately wanted to have her own apartment but knew that she could never afford to do so, particularly with the cost of day care. She didn't want to burden her mother and father any longer with all these extra responsibilities, but what choice did she have right now? She also knew it was becoming a little difficult at home since her mother was beginning to develop a closer relationship to her children than she was. This considerably concerned Nanette.

Then she heard of a new program to help with housing costs, and submitted her application. Within a few weeks, Nanette was approved. Now all she needed to do was find an adequate apartment that would also qualify her for the program. This was easier said than done – apartments were very hard to come by. In order for her to make it financially, she would have to continue to depend on her parents for help with childcare.

Nanette had enough time each morning to dress and feed her two sons before she had to be at work at 8:30 a.m. She often neglected herself in order to make sure her two sons were well taken care of before she had to leave. After hours and hours at work, tending to the heavy pressures of making decisions, Nanette would get home most days about 6:30 p.m. – in time to bathe and get her children ready for bed, after which she would eat her dinner that Ann had left for her. Ann and Lee always made sure the two little boys had a good dinner before Nanette got home – an act they took seriously and found pleasurable. Dinner had always been a time for family and this was like having their own little family again. Caring for Jake and Jamie was one more very loving and unselfish act they both enjoyed as they provided for these two little grandsons whom they both adored.

Although Nanette was dating, none of these men were marriage material, and yet she felt very pressured by her son that she try harder to find a new daddy. Nanette had joined a singles group and attended many of the dances and parties they held. She was actively dating three gentlemen and enjoying herself, but nonetheless could not picture herself married to any of them, much less provide father material to her two little sons.

It was that fall when the restaurant of the hotel acquired a new contract for pastries and desserts from the bakery they had used for years. This new contract now meant that Nanette would have to meet Bartlett Squires for the first time. There was something about him and within weeks he asked her out. Nanette was awed by his mild manner and the gentleman he was. They spent hours and hours together when she finally brought him home to meet the "family"!

Jake was very suspicious of other men Nanette brought home, not that there were many. She was very discrete about bringing home gentlemen friends she thought the boys might appreciate. Jake seemed a little less suspicious with Bart than with other men Nanette had for dinner, which made her a little less apprehensive. At five years old, Jake appeared to have a better sense of approval for Bart than she had seen him express previously. There was still a small doubt in Nanette's mind for the way her oldest son responded to this man.

Jamie, on the other hand, thought Mommy had handpicked this man just so he could have a new playmate. Bart had no children of his own and having been an only child had never been around any nieces or nephews of his own. Taking on two small children was a real challenge for Bart.

Nanette and Bart continued to see each other daily and frequently made plans for activities that would include the boys. Time moved along quickly and after four months, Bart proposed to Nanette. She accepted with the idea they would have a respectable engagement period. Ann and Lee Peters were not as overwhelmed with excitement as Nanette would have liked. However, after dating several men now and before her previous marriage to Sam, Nanette began to accept the fact that her family would be negative about anyone she wanted to marry.

Two years after their first meeting, Nanette and Bart were married. A wedding that made the front page of the local newspaper. Since Bart was such a prominent businessman in the community, it made perfect sense to publicize their wedding. After all what better way to market his business than to have a picture of the bride and groom cutting the wedding cake he and his staff had so gloriously built – a six-tiered cake with elegant trim of silver and gold beading and of course, real yellow and salmon roses encased the layers and sprawled around the entire cake table. A sight for only the most sophisticated of society – what else would the population of his town expect from this famous bakery of 50 years?

Their wedding made all the society pages since it was the most elaborate wedding anyone in this small New England town had ever heard of. Since Bart knew so much about the food industry, everything was spectacular from the two hours cocktail time, to the hand-carved roast beef by individual chefs and their assistants tableside, to the French desert table or rather room. Everything was absolutely amazing and Bart saw to every last detail paying for everything but Nanette's wedding gown and his wedding band -- the source of which she obtained from the sale of her first engagement ring to her mother. Nanette's two sons were dressed in the cutest of tuxedos and carried the wedding rings.

At the end of the wedding ceremony little Jamie looked up at his mother with his big eyes and said, "So, mommy, are we all Squires now?"

"Yes, honey we are all Squires now," replied Nanette. Although officially the little boys were not Squires, since they were moving to a new town, and were starting a new school system, Bart and Nanette agreed the boys would use his name. Their own father had totally estranged himself from them and was no longer any part of their lives.

Nanette and Bart spent the next two years in a peaceful, but stressful family and business life together raising the two boys and running the family bakery. Bart and Nanette seemed to work side by side together in the business even better than they were able to manage the household chores or their marriage.

"What's for dinner?" Bart asked

"I'm making chicken tonight."

"I don't want chicken. Can't you make anything worthwhile to eat?" barked Bart.

Each loved to cook and the kitchen was always a scene of frustration between the couple. Nanette usually gave in and let Bart cook so she could accomplish something with the boys or do something that needed attention at the bakery. With their townhouse apartment only four feet from the store and part of Bart's parents' house, it was easy for either of them to run back and forth from store to home. It did not, however, give much for separation between work and home for either of them.

The entire family was active in the bakery including the children. There were always things to do. Bart's parents created many beautiful breads, cakes, pies, cookies and pastries.

"You can't make a wedding cake using that much rum, Pop," explained Bart

"I can do whatever I want. It's my business," responded Stewart in his usually gruff voice.

"I will have to have another cake ready for the decorators when they discover the icing won't stay on these layers," Bart screamed. You make so much extra work and expense for me.

"Then leave. See if I care," Stewart would respond with his usual sarcastic attitude.

Just as Stewart and Bart were in this heated discussion again, a customer walked into the store.

"What do you want?" barked Stewart

The customer looked at Bart, who calmly walked over to her and politely asked her to sit at the counter and offered her a cup of fresh brewed coffee. This would have been another lost customer as Pop kept doing this to everyone who walked in the store.

Bart was continually irritated at the presence and aging abilities of his parents, but there was no way Bart and Nanette would be able to accommodate all the clientele they had acquired over the last 50 years without their help and ability to oversee the whole operation, certainly not the way the operation was being run currently. Stewart still held all the strings to the money until finally his health began to fail. Finally in desperation, and after almost ten years of Nanette's faithful devotion to the family business, Stewart begged her to help him manage the business. After some negotiations between the two, Stewart agreed to turn the business over to Bart and Nanette and to stay out of the everyday operations along with Debra. It would mean computerizing everything and perhaps hiring on more employees, but Nanette was sure they could cope better if they were computerized.

Besides the main store, there was a building attached in the rear which made breads of all kinds. These breads were a mainstay of the bakery.

People came from all over to buy these breads and many years ago, Bart and his father, Stewart had contracted with many local grocers to handle these products as well. The breads became a trademark of the "homemade" style of Squire's Bakery.

Ten years or so before Nanette came into the family, Bart and his father built a second building down near the railroad tracks where they made all sorts of pastries and cookies. This part of their business had grown over the years but not like their breads. The main bakery had been reserved for the making of cakes and pies. The operations employed more than 35 people in order to run all the various segments of the family bakery – no small enterprise for a family-owned business.

Selling all their products to local grocers was one thing, but Bart had recently introduced the shipment of fresh products to regional grocers as well. Having a banking and accounting background, Nanette oversaw the account receivables and payables of all parts of the business. Now this new concept brought an additional responsibly for her – to manage the shipment of these products, which proved to take a good deal of her time. Her plate was full as she also maintained all the payroll records (a job she reserved for evenings when she could focus and be alone to do so). She had joined Bart in many of the trade shows that offered training in various skills such as managing a business, to new styles of designs and product offerings. During these times, Nanette learned about cost accounting, merchandising, and marketing – all of which she took back to the business and implemented as many things as she could to help grow the business. The need for more and more employees grew as she began to have more and more outlets for their fresh "homemade" products.

Nanette had put in a long day spending more than twelve hours in the bakery's office doing paperwork. She still had payroll to do and was so exhausted. The orders kept coming in and shipments had to go out first thing in the morning. She had crews on all day and night to keep up with all the orders. Bart had been inside tending to dinner and although was not happy with putting the children to bed, had done so.

"Just what do you think you are doing?" asked Bart

"I've just finished getting all the invoices paid, the orders for the bread shipments are ready to be packaged at 5:00 a.m., and the 100 orders for pastries and cookies to be shipped at 6:00 a.m. Now I have to prepare the payroll for all the employees tomorrow," explained Nanette.

"Well do you realize I had to feed the boys and put them to bed myself? Are you ever going to be a mother to them?"

"Don't you dare throw that in my face. I'm there for them every day when they get home from school. It's me that helps them with their homework. It's me that cleans that house. You don't want me to cook any more – so I don't. You know if you'd prefer, you can pay someone to come in here and do what I do – and let your business fall on its face. I've made your business what it is today and you know it."

"Oh blah, blah, blah! I could do all this stuff blindfolded."

"Look, don't push me Bart. I'm in no mood for your crap."

"Yeah, what are you going to do – divorce me?"

With that Nanette got up and left, going into the house. Her responsibilities were overwhelming, growing every day, and consuming every part of her. Nanette continued to work hard to balance caring for her family and overseeing the business aspects of the family business. She knew that only by careful marketing of the business would they be able to stay competitive with all the local supermarkets now producing many fairly good quality products of their own. She had a niche that no one else had and she worked hard to achieve that.

"There seems to be a problem upstairs with the ceiling lights of one of our tenants," Bart told his father while Nanette was standing there counting orders. "I've ordered a part, but it is going to take a few weeks to come in."

"Did you tape up the wall switch?" asked Stewart.

"Yes, we should be fine."

Shortly after Stewart left to take Debra for coffee, the local insurance agent came into the store.

"Hi, Bart, Nanette. How are you two doing?" said Andy Cholla.

"We're good. Same old stuff, you know with Pop. He's always trying to run things."

"I thought you ought to know that he took the insurance off the building again today. He is claiming that because it is brick, it won't ever have a fire."

"Oh, Andy," exclaimed Bart. Put it right back on, immediately."

"Sure thing, Bart."

After Andy had left, Bart looked at Nanette with his usually frustration. "If Pop doesn't stop taking the insurance off the building, we are going to have a problem one of these days."

The main building housed as many as three other businesses that helped pay the property taxes and maintenance on all the properties. This was a part of the business that Bart himself handled and Nanette was glad to have one responsibility off her shoulders. Bart kept all the properties maintained and in good working order.

Several days later, Bart and Nanette got confirmation from their family doctor that they were about to have a child of their very own. Bart was so beside himself, he just wanted to tell the world.

"If we tell your mother first, my mother is going to have hurt feelings, and you know that, Bart," exclaimed Nanette.

"Okay. Let's plan a family dinner and have them all there. Then we can tell them all at once."

"Sounds like a plan."

During their wonderful celebration with both sets of parents, Bart and Nanette were a bit nervous at what their parents would say. After dinner, Bart and Nanette removed the dinner plates in preparation for dessert. There under each plate was the announcement of the new baby Squires to be born sometime the following May. Stewart and Debra Squires were the first to realize what the announcement said, but a big sigh from Ann Peters and a nudge from Lee soon told the whole table that the new baby would be a welcomed sight for everyone. Nanette and Bart were so relieved that everyone felt the tension relax. Jake and Jamie were not so delighted, as this meant that their mother, who was already quite busy trying to maintain the store and taking care of the house, that they had little time except for homework help to spend with their mother already. This would mean she would be even busier with a new baby – another person to take up her time.

Two days after this wonderful announcement, as Stewart and Debra were about to leave for their evening coffee, a habit they did every day, they noticed fire in one of the upstairs businesses. Total chaos broke out, as that was a particularly busy time for the bakery just before Thanksgiving. Many orders had already been made and everyone was in high production mode. The fire department was called and every employee was brought up to the main building to move orders that had been completed or started to a safe building or into the townhouse dining room before any smoke or water damage could ruin them. This was the beginning of Nanette's nightmare life.

The fire marshal threatened to shut down the bakery saying it was more than 50 percent burned and could not be reconstructed, as it was too old for the zoning requirements of the current day. Nanette watched as she saw her husband's personality change right under her nose. He managed to prevent losing the building but there was so much water damage on the other side of the building that they lost all their tenants – money that was so necessary to help with the expenses of maintaining all the properties.

The following morning Andy Cholla came into the bakery. "Bart are you aware that your father took off the insurance on the properties yesterday morning?"

"Andy, you have to be kidding me. Please tell me you are kidding me!" screamed Bart.

"I'm afraid not, Bart. You have no liability, theft, or fire insurance on any of the properties.

Bart was beside himself and now more than ever he had nowhere to turn. He turned now to liquor to help him cope with the inevitable consequences of his father's meddling.

A several million-dollar lawsuit had begun against the bakery and against all the Squires personally. Bart began to drink more than his usual, day in and day out. They were no longer able to make their payments for their products in cash and having enough to make payroll each week became more and more of a problem. Things seemed to go on a decline every day. After several weeks, Bart began to hit the children more and more frequently for absolutely no reason.

"That's enough, Bart. I forbid you to touch those boys ever again. You may have adopted them, but they are my flesh. Never lay a hand on them again," Nanette laid the law down to Bart in no uncertain terms. She was angry and her anger grew every day.

"Oh lay off. You're just making them sissies," barked Bart.

"Then they will be my sissies, won't they? Don't touch them, you hear," yelled Nanette in a tone that even the cats scurried away from.

The days were longer than ever and Nanette was due to have her baby shortly. The business was failing more and more every day, however she had to let the employees try to do the jobs she had been doing because she had to deliver a healthy baby. That was her main purpose now. She had hired a new bookkeeper and an office manager to handle some of the duties she had done, but the marketing aspect had just stopped entirely. Her ability to do the cost accounting, the displays, and the marketing were just going to have to wait until she got the new baby settled.

She delivered a third handsome and healthy baby boy – Theodore Jason Squire weighing in at nine pounds. He was a duplicate of his older brother Jake. They looked so much alike, except Teddy had brown eyes instead of the striking sky blue ones Jake had. She now had three boys – her very own three sons.

Nanette's life was never going to be the same. Every day she cared for little Teddy, Jamie and Jake like a mother was supposed to. Her focus was on her family and she totally didn't care whether Bart's business was doing well or not. He drank more and more every day. Even when she began to help him in the business, he barked at her so much, she lost all interest in doing so. After two years of the business deteriorating, Stewart begged Nanette to return to the bakery and continue her marketing efforts in order to turn things around. Teddy was now old enough to be put into a daycare facility and they would pay for the best in town. He would have a chance to socialize with children his own age. Nanette agreed and began to do her magic again.

However, the fights between her and Bart were more and more every day as Bart drank more and more. Most of the bad ones occurred in the house and away from the business. Then Bart began hitting Nanette and one evening after dinner when he was so drunk he could hardly stand, he beat Nanette in front of the children so badly she thought for sure her life was over. The older children ran for their grandparents who were able to stop Bart. This was all smoothed over by the family, and things began to run the same way again the next day, as if nothing had happened. Bart would be fine for a few days and then he would begin the drinking again. The beatings would start again, but, of course, this prominent family couldn't have their domestic lives aired publicly. Thus, Nanette kept taking it thinking she had to. Maybe she had irritated Bart and that it was all her fault, after all he kept telling her she was no good, so she must be no good. She began to think of herself as a terrible, horrible mother and person. Life was getting harder and harder for Nanette to endure.

Day after day, Nanette would cry alone to herself and her God above to take her from this horrible life and restore her to some sort of peaceful living. Surely the God she knew did not mean for her to live like this or to raise her sons in this environment.

After five years of this type of living over and over again, Bart's drinking, becoming drunk by noon, and violent by 6:00 p.m., Nanette felt enough was enough. Teddy came home from school one day in a fit of hysterics. He was going to kill himself if Nanette didn't do something about that man. Within one month, Nanette and her sons moved to a new apartment in a quiet neighborhood leaving behind the nightmare life that had existed every day for the last ten years. It wasn't over, but it was better.

God must have had a hand in this move because the landlord agreed to rent her the apartment if Jake, now nineteen years old, signed the lease. What a huge responsibility to put on a young man. The landlord also agreed to let her use the dining for a bedroom and the upstairs for her sons. There was a double driveway for all of their cars, and a big side yard for Teddy and the family to enjoy each other and their friends. There were children on this street for Teddy to play with and most of the folks on the street attended the local church where Nanette knew the Pastor and his wife. Jake was now working full time and putting himself through college. Jamie was about to graduate from high school. Both Jake and Jamie had their own cars and their own friends – most of who ended up sharing dinner with them over and over. It was a real turn of events and this family who had lived some trying times for several years were sharing some happy times. Would peace fall on them finally?

Chapter X

Introduction to Adult Independent Living Association (AILA)

Dr. Harkins knew of a program in a local community that he thought Pete might qualify for. He called the Adult Independent Living Association and began the paperwork to see if he could get Pete qualified for this program where he might be able to share an apartment with one or two other folks, but would have the assistance of a social worker to help him understand how to pay bills, do grocery shopping, cook meals and clean house. Dr. Harkins thought this would be a much better plan for Pete than to continue to live with his parents where too many things were being provided for him.

Ellie and Dan Gallagher were delighted with the news of this possibility for Pete. They did not want to think that when their days were over that Pete would not be able to carry on for himself. They knew he needed some kind of assistance, but had no idea that such a program existed nor that Pete might qualify. Would Pete be able to live on his own with this type of assistance? The Gallaghers were hopeful for the first time in many years.

Dr. Harkins made the calls to introduce Dan and Ellie Gallagher to Julie Laughlin, Director of the Adult Independent Living Association, also known as AILA. Julie was a slight built young woman who hardly seemed old enough to have finished high school much less have any knowledge about the needs of Pete Gallagher. Dan Gallagher was very skeptical of

Julie and this new program solely based on his first impression of this young woman.

"How wonderful to meet you, Mr. & Mrs. Gallagher. AILA is very proud of the services we are able to provide for adults that are struggling with everyday life. I will tell you, however, we do not have any other brain-injured folks in our Apartment Program, as it is my understanding is Pete's challenge. Am I correct?"

"Yes, that's correct," responded Ellie.

"Then how on earth can you possibly think you can help Pete," said Dan Gallagher, now in a very spiteful mood. He was very upset that Ted Harkins had brought them to this point.

"Now, dear, let's just listen to what Julie has to tell us before we get upset." Ellie Gallagher was just as annoyed but still held hope that there might be more to this than what they had just heard.

Julie Laughlin spent the next several hours explaining the programs that AILA offered. She took great patience to deliberate on the positives of learning how to grocery shop, prepare food and pay bills. She explained in great details how a social worker would supervise all activities of Pete's life in order for him to begin to learn to live independently, including monitoring a job situation.

"Now Dan and Ellie, if I may call you by your first names, I have to also remind you we cannot provide you with any guarantees that this Apartment Program will be successful for Pete," explained Julie. We have lots of mentally challenged folks who have benefited wonderfully from the program, but there are others who have not. Again, I have to also remind you that Pete would be our only brain-injured person; that most of our citizens are mentally challenged. You must also be aware that Pete would have to begin the program, as others have, in a group home.

Ellie Gallagher gasped so loudly her entire chair moved. For the first time Ellie broke her calm demeanor, "Absolutely not. I will not have our son living in a household of fifteen or twenty mentally challenged people.

I won't have it. I will not have it. That's all. I will not hear of it. Let's go Dan. We're done here. They can't help our Pete. They won't help our brain-injured son."

Dan Gallagher was the one to now calm the environment of this very lengthy and heated conversation. "We have to give this a try, Ellie. Pete can't continue like this. Julie, there must be some other way to introduce Pete into the Apartment Program.

"I know this is all new and can be overwhelming," Julie responded. "Let me see what I may be able to work out. We will have to meet with Pete and run some tests. We usually don't put our citizens in the Adult Independent Apartment Program with two or three roommates for a couple of years. However, since this is new to us also, let me meet with the folks from the Department of Social Services, the Department of Mental Retardation where Pete is getting his job coaching needs, and my colleagues here. Perhaps if Pete scores high enough on our battery of tests, perhaps he could start in the Apartment Program with a roommate or two. We usually like to pair up three people together, if possible. Give me some time to work on this, pull some additional resources, and run the tests with Pete."

"Oh," responded Ellie, "but I want a good living situation for our son. He's a good person and I only want the best for him." Ellie had all she could do to hold back the tears.

It took weeks to gather all the necessary research, test Pete, and consult with other professionals concerning this important step in Pete Gallagher's life. However, Pete Gallagher joined the Apartment Program two weeks before his 30th birthday.

It was a beautiful spring day when Pete moved into his first apartment with two other roommates. He was so hopeful. Life seemed to be looking up for Pete Gallagher. There were only a few things, as Pete never moved before so his worldly possessions consisted of his clothes and a few items from his childhood he just couldn't part with. His whole family was on hand to help make the move-in run as smoothly as possible bringing in a few items he held near and dear to him along with his clothes. His mother had rummaged through her kitchen to bring him a few of her "not-so-often used" pots and pans, a few dishes, glasses, and old mugs. Pete was on top of the world.

He met Sarah Archibald first. She lived in this town all of her life where Pete was now invading. Sarah felt resentful that Pete was now intruding on her space, and she was not so friendly to Pete on their first meeting.

"Who are you?" asked Sarah. "Why are they bringing in all this stuff?"

"I'm Pete Gallagher and I'm going to be your new roommate!" exclaimed Pete with all the enthusiasm he could muster.

"I don't need no new roommate," Sarah responded in her usual bad English.

"Well, you got one and it's me."

Julie Laughlin was quick to interject, "Sarah, of course you want a new roommate and Pete is just perfect for your household. He's nice and tall and can reach things when you need them. You won't have to climb that step stool every time something is too high up. You know, Sarah, he's not bad looking either and a great listener. I think you and Pete will enjoy living in this home together. Where is Steffan?"

"I don't know. He went out this morning he said for coffee. I don't know why he has to go out for coffee when we have a coffee pot and coffee right here. Maybe he needs to get away from me. I know he thinks I'm stupid."

"You're not stupid, Sarah," said Julie. Steffan has his buddies he likes to visit with at the coffee shop and he probably went there to have his coffee and visit with his friends. I'm sure it has nothing to do with you. Pete, you'll get to meet Steffan later."

"Steffan Lewinski had lived in Poland before coming to the United States," explained Julie. "He too is mentally challenged, as is Sarah. Steffan and Sarah were both deemed as 'high-functioning' mentally challenged citizens. Steffan is very capable but his speech gets in his way. He spent many years living in Maine and only came to New England a couple of years ago when his sister and brother-in-law moved here. He does hold a job washing dishes at the local prep school. He means well but has quite a temper, so be careful Pete. Don't purposely tease him; he really has no sense of humor."

Sarah Archibald watched as each piece of Pete's things was brought in and items place in the common areas. She was very resentful that she was going to have to share this house with yet another roommate. Over the last six months there had been eight different people move in and move out, now this tall person with all his "tall" things was moving in. Sarah watched with such a suspicious eye and when she could not stand it anymore she just had to interfere.

"Hey what's with all the hats? How many hats does one person need? You can only wear one hat. Why do you have to have so many hats?"

"I like hats. I like to wear hats so I won't lose my hair," explained Pete. I wear a different hat depending on where I'm going and whom I'm going to be with. I like to collect hats like some people collect baseball cards or dolls."

"I don't collect dolls or baseball cards. Collecting things is stupid. It just means you have to dust more things. You're stupid to have so many hats. You're stupid, Pete Gallagher, stupid."

"Sarah Archibald!" exclaimed Julie. "Apologize to Pete. That is no way to start your living arrangement. That was not a nice thing to say to Pete."

"No, I'm not sorry. I don't want another person living in this house and I think he is stupid to have so many hats."

"Sarah, apologize to Pete."

"No." And with that Sarah stomped off to her room to leave the rest in a state of amazement. What was this living arrangement going to mean for Pete?

Once all of Pete's things were in and placed where he wanted them, his bed made and his worldly possessions placed according to his wishes, his few kitchen items packed away, his family said their good-byes and left Pete to contemplate meeting Steffan and try to understand how he would deal with Sarah and her moods. Julie Laughlin stayed with Pete for several hours hoping to be at home when Steffan returned so she could help any negative impact the meeting of the two men might encounter. However, Julie had other tasks she needed to accomplish and had to leave Pete to fend for himself and try to ward off any negative vibrations from Steffan.

After more than six hours later and Pete exhausted from his day, he decided to call it a day and went to take a nap in his room. Steffan Lewinski still had not returned home. It was morning before Pete awoke to find Steffan starring down on top of him. Steffan was a large Polish fellow with a head of hair enough for two people. His had a full body and whether it was muscle or fat, Pete was not sure, he just knew that Steffan was a lot bigger man than he was and he didn't want him landing on top of him. Steffan was as short as Pete was tall, but certainly made up for it in his roundness.

"Hello, you must be Steffan?" Pete asked.

"Yeah, what's it to you and why are you in this room?"

"This is my room now. I'm your new roommate. I moved in yesterday. I'm sorry we didn't meet yesterday but you were out."

"Whatever! You here for longer than a week or are you a fast sweep to check out the digs like all the rest of them?"

"Don't understand. What do you mean?"

"They come, they go, they fight, they argue, they leave shit everywhere and I don't like living with a different person every day. That's what I mean."

"I expect to stay here for a long time, Steffan. It will probably depend on how well we can all get along."

"See, I told you. Another one of them coming to see what we are doing every day," poked Sarah.

"Get out of here. This is a man's bedroom and no place for a female to be uninvited." Steffan was not happy with Sarah at that moment, but that was the way Sarah was, always putting her nose into other people's business.

"It's my house too and I have a right to be anywhere I want to be."

"Out of here, woman or I'll put you out," Steffan was downright angry now.

"No."

With one fell swoop, Steffan picked up the tiny Sarah and proceeded to carry her out of Pete's bedroom and dropped her on the sofa in the living room.

"Stay out of Pete's room or I'll put you out in the mud."

"You wouldn't dare."

"Don't push me, Sarah!"

Steffan and Sarah continued to banter day after day with Pete. He appeared to be their latest pong in a dangerous game of roommate against roommate. The tension mounted more and more each day. Pete did everything in his power to stay out of their way feeling as though he had entered a lion's den.

In spite of the situation between those he lived with, Pete began to learn more and more about living independently from his family. With the aid of Julie Laughlin, he and his roommates began to learn how to prepare a weekly meal plan. From this meal plan, which the three tenants had to share and agree upon, yet another challenge for Pete, they would derive their grocery list. However, Pete had lots of difficulties remembering his meal plan and/or his grocery list. He had to remember, yet again, to bring his list with him when it was time to shop. One more issue to cause tension between Steffan, Sarah and Pete. Although this should have been a fairly simple thing for Pete to learn, his brain injury made it far from simple.

From one week to the next, Pete found himself in a constant argument with his co-tenants. He would argue with them for the need of an item at the apartment for which they probably had more than they already needed or could use. Pete became very frustrated with this aspect of sharing his life with people he was having a difficult time getting to know. They constantly argued with him and between themselves.

Once a month, Julie would come by to help each of them to pay their share of all the bills associated with living at the house. That meant that for the first time in his life, Pete had to learn how to write a check, balance a checkbook, and make deposits. Although Pete liked numbers and had been very good at numbers, remembering the things he should was a difficult task. Simple things such as adding and subtracting became a huge problem for Pete. Additionally, he had to remember to put all his entries in his checkbook – one more thing to remember.

All of these things were compounded by the terrible tension created by his roommates. Every time one of them raised their voices, Pete thought the inside of his head would explode. If the memory problems were not enough for Pete to contend with, his entire personality changed each time a new fight or disagreement came about. He became a different person. He acted like he escaped from a mental institution and Pete was well aware that things were not right, but he just didn't know how to express his feelings and to whom. He found himself going outside often to have another cigarette or just take a walk to get his head straightened out again. The tension of this new living arrangement made Pete wonder if this was the way things were really supposed to be.

The days grew longer and longer as Pete struggled with trying to maintain his job with Constructive Workshop where he had a job coach, to do the everyday things required to maintain his own life. He was full of anxiety from morning to night. Apprehension prevented Pete from complaining to anyone of his feelings for fear they would make him go back to the institution to live for the rest of his life. Someway, somehow,

Pete had to learn how to deal with all the things that challenged him every day. If this was the way he was supposed to live, he really wasn't sure he wanted to stay in this world at all. Thoughts of ending his life became more and more frequent.

Pete became more and more challenged on his part-time job. He was having increasing episodes of remembering what to do, complaining to his job coach about the people he had to work with day in and day out (all of whom were mentally challenged), and complaining to Julie about how his boss was so lazy, that he never did any work.

It wasn't long before the thoughts of ending his life kept creeping into Pete's mind over and over again. One Wednesday morning after the typical banter going on between Sarah and Steffan, Pete decided to take more of his medication than he knew was prescribed. Sarah and Steffan both left for work and Pete was left to fend for himself, however, he knew he would soon leave this world and wouldn't have to deal with any of his problems ever again.

This was, however, the day that Julie Laughlin decided she needed to visit Pete earlier than usual and stopped by the apartment minutes after Steffan and Sarah had left. She found Pete lying on the floor of the bathroom and called for emergency help. Within minutes Pete was rushed to the local hospital and his family was called. Pete spent several hours in the Emergency Room and was admitted to the psychiatric ward of the hospital. After two weeks he was sent back to the institution where he had lived previously for four years for additional observation for another two months. Dr. Harkins was very sure that the living situation might have been a bit harsh, but that Pete would adjust given time. He suggested and agreed to see him every day for the next several weeks.

Six months after Pete's attempted suicide, Steffan confronted Pete about his buying habits.

"You're always buying too many things. We have enough hand soap, toilet paper and toothpaste to last a lifetime," quipped Steffan.

"We can always use them," said Pete.

"Hey, I'm not working here to pay for a lifetime of your needs," said Steffan.

"You're using the stuff, too," Pete barked back.

"Like I don't need your crappy toothpaste. Stop buying it. I don't like it."

Pete couldn't handle the loud voice of Steffan and his other personality began to emerge. Steffan thought that Pete was play-acting and that aggravated him even more. The banter continued until finally Steffan began to physically beat on Pete until Pete was unable to move.

"I don't care what you like. Be glad I'm doing most of the shopping," Pete attempted to respond after having his breathe knocked out of him.

With that comment, Steffan pushed Pete against the wall. Pete was so stunned he just stood there for a minute.

"Look man, you'd better do what I tell you or you'll be in a big trouble," shouted Steffan in a huge brusque voice.

Now Pete was angry and pushed back. What a big mistake. Steffan swung a punch into Pete's stomach that set him sailing across the room through the chairs of the kitchen table and landing his head against the metal back door.

Steffan continued to scream about Pete's habits of buying too much, spending too much and not paying his share of the bills.

Sarah came flying into the apartment from her job to find Pete lying flat on the kitchen floor in a puddle of blood. She panicked and screamed at the top of her lungs. Her screams could be heard for blocks away. José Quinta, the landlord for this threesome's apartment, rushed through the door and immediately tried to get Pete to come to. He urgently dialed 911 for emergency assistance. José worked and worked on Pete, and although he was still breathing, he wasn't moving. Within minutes the paramedics and ambulance, preceded by several policemen were on the scene. Pete was rushed to the local city hospital where the doctors worked on him for hours and hours.

Thanks to the quick reaction of José, his attention to Pete, his notification to AILA and their notification to the family, everyone was at Pete's side within minutes of his injuries. After several hours in surgery to repair a ruptured spleen, internal bleeding, and some serious injuries to his left leg and foot they emerged to give the news to his family that Pete would survive his ordeal. He would need several months to heal, lots of physical therapy and maybe more surgeries on his leg and foot. He would, however, heal and return to his normal self with lots of TLC.

Dan and Ellie Gallagher decided at that moment that Pete would come back home and they would pull him out of the AILA Program. They were beside themselves that this had happened to Pete after he had already suffered so much in his young life. They also knew he was facing more surgery on his left leg and foot with the strong possibility of losing a toe this time. He would need more dedicated care living at home with his parents. Now they would have to regroup and develop another plan for Pete -- something they could all live with. Pete's life was about to change again – would he ever lead a "normal" life like his parents?

Chapter XI

Re-Introduction to Independent Living

The days and weeks ahead for Pete Gallagher were difficult. It was bad enough that he was in such awful pain from all his injuries, but now he was living back home with his parents. This is not what he wanted. He had hoped he could live like a somewhat normal person on his own.

He had to have a toe removed, his small toe replaced and surgery on his left leg. Now several months of living at home recovering from all these injuries and Pete was ready to try to live on his own again.

"Please, Mom, please talk to Dad and let me try the Apartment Program again," pleaded Pete. "Maybe I just got the wrong roommates and maybe different people would work better."

"They are only going to want to put you in a group home and I won't hear of that. You are not mentally challenged, Pete and I am not having my son put in with a lot of people who are. People will just perceive you as mentally challenged then."

"Mom, I don't care. What I care about is learning how to live on my own. I want my own life. I want to learn how to take care of myself, have a job, and get married someday with my own family."

"Now, Pete. You know better than that. You are never going to be able to support a wife and a family. You need to get that notion right out of your head. You're never going to get married. Don't even get your father started on that idea. He'll never agree to letting you get back into the Apartment Program with that attitude."

"Okay, okay, but please Mom, won't you just talk to Dad about getting me back into the AILA Program, please?"

"Okay, okay. He'll be home from his trip on Friday. I'll try to talk to him over the weekend."

Pete thought Friday would never come and he was so anxious to get back out on his own. A small taste of learning to shop for groceries, make his own meals, have his own checking account and paying his own bills, just like his parents did, was just such a dream – a dream he felt he could achieve if he just put his mind to it.

Two days later on Wednesday afternoon, Julie Laughlin called Ellie Gallagher.

"Mrs. Gallagher, this is Julie Laughlin from AILA. I really would love to have the opportunity to talk to you and Dan about Pete re-joining the group. It was a very bad mistake that happened and I don't think we did a good job in pairing up Steffan and Sarah with Pete. There is, however, an opening with two guys that I think Pete would really get along with just fine," Julie pleaded with Ellie.

"I don't know, Julie. My husband and I are very upset with the horrible beating he got at the hands of one of your 'citizens'," responded Ellie. "We just don't think this is a good thing for Pete, who is brain injured to be around folks who are mentally challenged. They can't possibly understand Pete and we know Pete can't understand them. This may be a very bad idea to even consider for Pete."

"Please, Mrs. Gallagher. Please give the Program and AILA another chance to prove you wrong," exclaimed Julie. We did make some mistakes and we'd really like to make things right for Pete and all of you. Please think about it. Talk to Dan and Pete and get back to me next week. If you like, I'd be more than willing to come to your home to talk to you and Dan. I really think this new home would be so much better for Pete.

Ellie Gallagher was caught between wanting what was best for her son and also a safe place to have him learn life skills. She did not want to subject him to another beating and more injuries or to entertain more thoughts of suicide; he had enough of that. She also knew that neither she nor her husband were getting any younger and they needed to get Pete settled in life somehow. What would happen to their son if he didn't know how to take care of himself or didn't have some of the resources that might be available to him? He would have no idea how to go about providing these things for himself. She also felt a sense of guilt in laying all this on one of her other children should something happen to her and/or Dan. They had a right to their own lives and their own families. She didn't want to burden them with Pete and his difficulties.

After weeks of Ellie speaking to Dan about Pete re-joining the AILA Program, he finally agreed to talk to Julie Laughlin again. A meeting was arranged but did nothing to convince Dan to change his mind.

"Mr. Gallagher, please consider letting us pair Pete up with these two fellows who are just wonderful people. They are very mellow and do not have the bad temper or the explosive nature that Steffan and Sarah had," pleaded Julie Laughlin.

Dan Gallagher was a very stubborn and proud man and was determined that his son would stay living at home where they could provide for him properly. This was his son and he felt very protective of Pete and his wellbeing.

"I do not think this is a wise decision, Julie," said Dan. "I stretched my inner feelings to let you come here to talk about this to us, but I cannot sleep with myself if I even thought I was putting my son in harm's way. The answer is no and that is all I have to say on the subject. You are welcome to stay and have coffee but this discussion is over." With his last comment, Dan Gallagher removed himself from the two ladies and let Ellie deal with the fallout of his comments.

Then one morning out of nowhere, Dan Gallagher came out to the kitchen where Ellie was busy preparing the Saturday morning breakfast for the family.

"You know, Ellie, I've been thinking. Pete is getting older and maybe he won't be able to learn as easily about the things of life as he ages. Maybe we ought to meet these two young men they want to pair Pete up with. Maybe that would make a difference in the way we think about having Pete rejoin the Apartment Program," said Dan. "Maybe being in the AILA Program will teach Pete the life lessons that we just can't do here. They seem to be more experienced and trained in the social services that Pete needs."

"You mean it, Dan?"

"Yeah, let's invite them for dinner so we can get to know these two young fellows," said Dan. "Don't mistake my comments, Ellie. I'm not giving you my blessing here on this decision. I am just trying to be more open minded and realistic about the situation we are facing."

Accompanied by Julie Laughlin, Blake Cavenelli and Phil Macintosh came for dinner the following Sunday. Both Ellie and Dan Gallagher were so impressed with the polite gentlemen they were, they hardly thought of them as mentally challenged at all. Pete took to the two guys like any other young men might and they went off to his room where Pete showed them all kinds of ribbons and trophies he had won before his injury – things he was so proud of, but no one before seemed to care. Blake and Phil cared and enjoyed talking with Pete for hours.

Within the next month, plans had been made for Pete Gallagher to re-join the Apartment Program, get reacquainted with a new job at Goodwill, and moved into the apartment that Blake and Phil shared. All three men seemed to get along so well, and everyone helped each other. They were a three-some and for the first time, Pete began to feel as though he had a home and a couple of real friends who really cared about him. These guys became a very important part of Pete's life. Life was good.

Julie came by the apartment every week to help the three guys pay their share of bills, put together a grocery list so they could shop now on their own, and make meals from that list – a job Pete was getting better at but was not happy about. Julie also worked with the three fellows in sharing the jobs of cleaning the house, taking out the trash, and doing laundry. They all seemed to care about pulling their own weight and all did their jobs according to the way Julie would set up the chore lists. Things were running smoothly for Pete for the first time in his life since his injury. He was making more and more friends through AILA, and becoming more and more involved in their social structure as well. He also was making friends at work although he didn't do much with them socially.

On one of Julie's visits, neither Blake nor Phil was home. So Julie did her usual things with Pete, making out the meal and grocery lists and splitting up the chore list. All of which were left on the refrigerator. She sat and talked with Pete for a long time. She found out he liked to play cribbage and made a date to do so on her next visit. She also understood that Pete was lacking a large part of his "old" life – his church life. It was during this meeting that Julie asked Pete if he would like to go to her church with her on Sunday – a Congregational church which was the type of church that Pete had grown up in. Pete agreed.

It was a beautiful sunny April day when Pete joined Julie for services at the Community Congregational Church. Everyone with lots of smiles greeted him and no one seemed to give him any strange looks, as he was so accustomed to. He joined Julie and her husband in the pew and watched as the choir marched in. There she was. What a striking woman. She sang in the choir who faced the congregation. She was in the front row. Pete wondered about this woman all through the service. She was a large, blonde woman but she was so striking. Then he would remember what his parents told him about the fact that he could never get married, so don't even think about trying to date women. He liked women, but this particular woman had really caught his eye. After the service, Julie introduced Pete to many of the other folks in church. Here she came down the aisle. Julie introduced Pete to Nanette Squires, who seemed as interested in meeting him as petting a snake. She passed by him with little to nothing to say, just a nod. This was the first person that seemed to give him even a hint of rejection. The one person he would like to get to know better. Maybe she's married and Pete was just misinterpreting her body language.

Pete began to interact with a new community of people – people who didn't see him for his weaknesses but instead for his strengths. He began to understand how to communicate and enjoy the company of people of all different walks of life the way other folks did. Now he finally began to have a different life – one much more like he saw his family have. He began to attend regularly to this new church and became active in some of the social activities. He began to have a more fulfilling social life and enjoyed not being home alone every evening. The evening had dragged along much of the time with only his job and the television as his constant companions. His other fellow workers were hard to talk to and he didn't find anything in common with them. That left Pete to his television friends whom he did talk to constantly but who just didn't answer him back. It wasn't long before Pete joined the church and was asked to serve on committees.

Although Pete was very articulate, the members of the various committees sometimes had trouble understanding that Pete's brain injury could prevent him from doing anything.

"Pete, I need you to remember to put out the traffic cones every Sunday at least 45 minutes before service," said Andy Cummings one of the members of the Prudential Committee.

"No, problem, Andy," said Pete. I can do that without any problem.

However, the following Sunday, Pete arrived at church in time for services and had totally forgotten to arrive early enough to put out the cones. Another member of the Prudential Committee had arrived about 30 minutes before service and saw they were not out yet, so he did them.

By Choice

"What happened to you this morning, Pete?" asked Andy Cummings. "Did you oversleep?"

"No, why," said Pete.

"You were supposed to put out the traffic cones 45 minutes before service."

"I was," said Pete. "I'm sorry. I'll do that next week for sure."

"Ok, but please remember to get here early enough to do so."

The next week Pete remembered and got the cones out. The following week he forgot and Andy reminded him again. The next two weeks Pete remembered fine, and the following week he forgot. This routine continued week after week. It was frustrating for Andy Cummings and the other members of the Prudential Committee. They continued to be patient with Pete and tried to give him every opportunity in order to feel he was participating and doing his part for the church. Pete wanted to be needed and wanted to help in any way he could, he just had lots of difficulty remembering to do the tasks that were given to him. If he forgot to write down every task in his little calendar book, more than likely he would forget in as little as one hour of being asked to do something. This frustrated Pete also, because he just wanted to be like the other guys – normal.

Nanette Squires had started to attend the Community Congregational Church a year before Pete with her son, Teddy after she had an automobile accident. She had suffered some serious whiplash and was not able to drive the car for some time, wearing a neck brace for several months. Nanette had brought Teddy to this church as many of the folks on the street attended this church and the Pastor and his wife were people she knew. Once she had begun to attend, getting rides from neighbors, she realized she knew a lot of the other members and Teddy went to school with many of the kids who were in Sunday School. Nanette wanted to make sure Teddy had the same Christian upbringing that his brothers had at the

Baptist Church where she, her entire family, and her two older sons had attended for years.

Nanette was also very much in the throngs of getting over the terrible divorce between her and Bart. He gave her a bad time about which one of them would raise Teddy, where he would live, who would make decisions for him, and what was best for Teddy. In the end, Nanette won on every count due to Bart's terrible track record of drinking too much and being seen publicly in such a state. She was dealing with a lot of issues still very raw and real. Meeting a man in church who appeared to have something wrong with him was not her idea of a positive future. She was overwhelmed and had a lot on her plate. She now was working two jobs, trying her best to take care of Teddy, and still keep the household chores up. She was dedicated to what needed to be done and adding anything else was not in the picture right now. She was fortunate to be able to sing in the choir and occasionally Teddy would come to rehearsals with her and sing on Sunday mornings also.

The months moved along slowly for Pete with the hopes of getting to know Nanette better. He found out that she had a son and had gone through a divorce. He knew very little more until the church began to form small groups. The Community Congregational Church had publicized to the congregation that they were going to hold a "lay witness weekend" where all the members would be included. It was attended by almost everyone and started from Friday evening with a potluck supper, worship, and some lay leaders who were brought in to lead the discussion and bible study efforts. It continued Saturday morning with breakfast at various members' homes and more leadership through discussions. These sessions continued throughout Saturday and into the evening with a catered dinner. Teddy got a chance to meet Pete in one of these small groups, which changed things for Pete without ever knowing what was happening. Teddy got a chance to hear about Pete's life and understood how being different for him must have felt since Teddy felt different also. He had always attributed his feelings to the fact that his brothers were eight and ten years older and that he had an alcoholic father. Now meeting Pete gave a very insight to Teddy and he felt a connection that was different than he had felt with the other members of the small group.

Then on one fateful day in March of the following year, Pete got a phone call from his mother that she wanted him to come over to the house. He arrived within the next hour and found that most of his family was already there. Pete wondered what was wrong. His brother told Pete that their father, Dan Gallagher, had been killed in an automobile accident. Pete was beside himself and couldn't talk for several minutes. He completely fell apart. Dan Gallagher had been his friend, not just his father. They had traveled together, gone fishing together, had delivered his papers together, had played golf together and so many other things. This had to be a bad dream. His pal couldn't be dead. No, not his Dad – not his buddy – not the guy who made things tough but also was his best friend in the entire world. It took Pete months and months to try to cope with the death of his father.

Months after the death of his father, Pete was still struggling with the loss of his best friend. He seemed to be coping with his Dad's death, but was having a lot more trouble remembering things than he had remembered previously. Again, Pete overdosed on his medication, and again was found by Julie. This time was deemed an accidental overdose because Pete didn't remember that he had already taken his meds for the day and had doubled up on his medication that morning. The hospital kept Pete for a week for observation under the guidance of Dr. Harkins. Again, Dr. Harkins began to see Pete every day for the next couple of months. It was very evident to everyone, however, that this was purely a memory problem and not a deliberate act. Dr. Harkins got Pete into a research program being offered at a local college under the guidance of another doctor, Dr. Sally Rigley. Her new research was helping brain-injured folks to try to use another part of their brain to help with short-term memory. Pete entered the Apartment Program within the next week, which proved to help him almost immediately.

While Pete was dealing with the death of his father, Nanette was dealing with the backlash of her divorce from Bart and trying to raise Teddy who was still in his developmental years. Jake and Jamie seemed to have moved into adulthood overnight and had developed lives of their own.

Jake had moved in with a friend in order to "house sit" for his friends' parents while they were trying to sell their home. He had moved from his banking job to working now for a law firm as a law clerk. He also attended college on an almost full-time schedule – his days were plenty full.

Jamie was working full time but still having difficulties deciding what he wanted to do. He had met Candice Satelli at his job and was very smitten with her. She was such a quiet little lady and seemed to make him very happy. He spent most of his free time with Candice. She convinced him to enter a community college and take a couple of courses while he was making his decision. Candice was in her second year of college at the time and she and Jamie seemed to enjoy each other's company, had a lot in common, and spent a good deal of time together.

Both the older boys had little time at home leaving just Nanette and Teddy living in the apartment. Nanette was working two jobs – a full-time one at a law firm as a legal secretary and three evenings and Saturdays as a front desk clerk for a local hotel. Unfortunately, that left Teddy to deal with his own dinner many nights and alone through the evenings. It was during this period of time when Teddy met a young lady and fell head over heels for her. Although Nanette didn't approve of Teddy seeing a young woman many years older than he was at the time, she also knew it was one way for Teddy to have some company and not be alone so much of the time. He joined her family many nights for dinner and the evening while she was still at work.

Only a few short months after Teddy met Connie Daley, Connie called Nanette at the hotel hectically and not knowing what to do – Teddy had begun to have pseudo seizures. After many ambulance trips to the hospital, seeing several doctors and specialists, lots of counseling, and medication it was finally determined that Teddy remembered some frightening abusive attacks from his childhood. Thanks to the brain specialist at Yale-New Haven Hospital, Teddy revealed some very personal experiences from his childhood. She explained to Teddy and Nanette that his seizures were happening because his body wanted the memories to come out. The only way the body could make that happen was to create a seizure. She felt that the seizures would stop in time and let Teddy leave the hospital without any medication.

Since all of Nanette's family and friends were afraid to handle Teddy (now a very large fourteen-year old), she had to take a family medical leave to care for Teddy and to fight with the school system to get him some home tutoring and schooling. It was a fight that Nanette worked on for years ahead until finally at sixteen years old she signed the papers for Teddy to leave school. Teddy experienced horrible migraines almost daily when he attended school. He wasn't advancing due to feeling sick so many days. Teddy did get work and worked at many various retail jobs, some successfully and some not so successful. Connie had been dedicated to staying with Teddy and being there to help him every step of his ordeal. After several years, Teddy and Connie decided to move in together with the intensions of planning a wedding.

Jamie decided to take a job on a cruise ship and Candice was broken hearted, but waited for months while he did what he wanted to and making some decisions about his own life in the process.

Pete continued to attend church every Sunday and although he thoroughly enjoyed the services, the other members, and doing volunteer work serving on some committees, he silently hoped that one day Nanette would notice him. He continued to live with Blake and Phil successfully until Julie came by one day and informed Pete that there was a beautiful new apartment that she thought he was ready to have on his own and live independently. Pete couldn't believe his ears. He was so delighted and felt so good about where he life was headed. This was a real advancement for Pete. His own place – his own home – a place he could take care of and call his place. So Pete Gallagher moved up the street to his own apartment that September and couldn't be happier to be on his own. He continued to see Blake and Phil and do lots of social things with his two special friends as well as many of the social activities provided by AILA.

Nanette continued to work hard on her two jobs, but found time to be part of the choir at church and to serve on the Board of Deacons. She had no difficulty meeting new people or having things to do. She made the decision before her car completely died, she would apply for a mortgage and try to buy her very first house – her own house. After months of paperwork, she closed on her house in December two days after the church Christmas party where she "saw" Pete Gallagher for the first time and gave this man a chance to express who he really was. They talked about a possibility for Pete to come see her new home.

Nanette shared her experience with Teddy about getting to know Pete Gallagher from church. Teddy was well aware of who Pete was and encouraged his mother to invite him for dinner – that he really was a very nice man and that she could feel very comfortable having him in her home. Teddy and Connie planned a "housewarming party" for his mother and included Pete in the invitation list. However, Pete Gallagher did not have a memory for names, and when he received the invitation he promptly threw it in the trash. Nanette was so hurt by Pete not responding that she decided she would not invite him to Jamie's graduation from college and that she didn't have time for someone who couldn't even respond to such an important part of her life. Teddy and Connie had to continually keep telling her that he was brain injured and tried to make Nanette understand that Pete probably didn't remember who she was. They tried to convince her to invite him for dinner by herself. After weeks and weeks of discussing the situation with Nanette, she finally agreed to invite Pete for dinner.

She thought she would plan a simple meal and get this over. Pete arrived on a Friday evening at 5:45 p.m. expecting to see many other folks from church there.

"Oh, Pete, I am so sorry. Did you need a ride?" exclaimed Nanette

"No, I took the bus. That's okay," responded Pete.

Nanette knew the bus stop was a mile from her house and that Pete walked with a limp. Her heart sank and she felt so horrible that she had asked this man to dinner without thinking about how he would travel more than fifteen miles to get to her house.

"Oh, Pete, I am so very sorry," Nanette cried out holding her hands over her heart in such compassion.

"That's okay," responded Pete. "I have my truck on the road!"

Nanette's heart sank again as she realized the humor he had just played on her. From that moment on, she immediately was at ease with Pete Gallagher. He had the same sense of humor that she had been raised with from her father and that her brother displayed. She was going to get along just fine with this man.

As Pete Gallagher entered her home, he saw a beautiful table set for two with candles, flowers, a tablecloth and china. His heart began to beat faster than he thought possible. He assumed this was a church function and that other members of the church would be attending this dinner. That was apparently not the case and for a brief moment he began to panic. He had not been asked to attend a dinner party with a lady like this too many times in his life and he was taken back for a few brief moments.

"Can I help, Nanette?" Pete asked. "Would you like me to make us some drinks?"

"That would be perfect," she answered. "I bought us some Johnny Walker Black as we had both mentioned we had a liking for."

Pete saw the liquor and glasses on the counter and began to fix the drinks as he watched Nanette prepare a tray of several hors d'oeuvres that impressed him beyond recollection. They moved into her living room and sat on the sofa together to enjoy their drinks and hors d'oeuvres. Pete could not believe this was happening to him. He was having an evening with the lady of his choice and by her invitation. The plate of hors d'oeuvres in front of him was just the beginning of what must be in her plans for their evening. Could he just pinch himself and see if he was really alive?

Pete got to know a lot more about Nanette and she got to know a lot more about Pete. They enjoyed a magnitude of laughter and Pete thought perhaps she had forgotten about dinner. Then out of nowhere, she excused herself and told him that dinner was being served in the dining room. How did she do that? She just produced this wonderful dinner of chicken, potatoes and corn and then to top all that off a beautiful desert. She was magic – cooking seemed to be no effort and they both had lots of time for conversation without it all being mixed up with preparations for dinner. How *did* she do that?

Nanette got up to clear the dinner dishes and Pete, as was his custom, followed suit. He came up behind her, swung her around and placed a passionate kiss on her soft lips. Nanette thought she would melt right there. This couldn't be happening – not again! She had to stay in control, she was not ready for any romantic relationship; just friends she told herself. He apologized when he saw her reaction and she turned again, looking up into his tall face and returned yet another kiss.

Would this be the beginning of something Pete had hoped for all his life? Was Nanette ready for what might be a challenge she wasn't prepared to handle?

Chapter XII

The Challenges of So Much Baggage

Nanette and Pete were certainly smitten with each other. They continued to talk to each other for hours at a time on the telephone. The week after the *famous* dinner-for-two, Pete entertained Nanette in his apartment. Nanette was so nervous to go to a "man's" apartment all by herself. This was a huge test for her due to the fact that she was brought up in such a strict Christian home; doing something like this would have certainly made her parents very upset. Yet Nanette knew she was a grown woman and had a mind of her own. She knew the values she was taught and grown up with. She also knew she was forced by two husbands to do things she never wanted to do. On her way to Pete's apartment she continually kept hearing the voice of Teddy telling her what a gentleman Pete was and that he would never do anything to hurt her. She was truly depending on her eighteen-year old son's opinion of a man she didn't know a whole lot about.

Nanette arrived at Pete's home and he greeted her with his usual sense of humor. Nanette took one look at his kitchen and into his living room and she knew immediately that this man had somebody looking out for him. He must have a family who supports him and makes sure he lives a decent life. He took her on the grand tour of his one-bedroom apartment and although he had only a few things, everything was tidy and immaculate. Someone was making sure this *man* had the skills to care for himself. Nanette was impressed so far. The décor of the apartment was so homey and comfortable and Pete made her feel right at home. Pete had not started dinner and asked her what she would like. This was different than the meal she had prepared for him. The meal was small and brief and Nanette made a decision at that very moment that she would do most of the cooking, if this relationship was going to continue. Pete Gallagher was not a cook – that was not one of his talents – and Nanette was not going to put Pete through this ordeal again.

They continued to meet and attend church together every Sunday morning and talked every day on the phone. Once or twice a week they got together to talk, have coffee, or if Nanette was flush with cash they might actually see a movie together. This was by far not the typical relationship. Pete only had enough money to pay his bills, buy what he needed for groceries, and gas for his truck. Nanette had a good job and even a second job. She occasionally was able to find more cash for them to enjoy a few moments of a "real date" now and then.

One night after working a long day, and a night shift at another job, Nanette called Pete before leaving to go home. He pleaded with her to come to his apartment for a short visit. He would make her a cup of tea and they could share some time for a short while. He knew she needed to get some much-needed sleep in order to face her challenges of the next day. Nanette drove almost twenty miles to Pete's apartment.

"Pete, put your coat on and come quickly. You have to see what I have just witnessed!" shouted Nanette in an enthusiastic exclamation of excitement.

"What is it?" asked Pete.

"I can't tell you, you just have to come and see."

Pete grabbed his coat and hat and headed out the door with Nanette in the cool night air. He looked, but could not see what Nanette saw.

"Pete, it was the largest full moon I have ever seen. It looked like it was about a mile from earth it was so large," Nanette explained in an excitement Pete had never seen before. "Come on, we have to take the car and go find it up on the hill."

Pete went and locked his apartment and joined Nanette in her car. They drove up the hill to see this full moon. It was everything she said it was. They parked the car on the side of the road and spent almost an hour admiring this huge full moon. They talked and talked non-stop with excitement over the moon, the weather, the day, and all sorts of things. Nanette had energy that Pete was sure would do him in. Where did she get all this energy from after working two jobs and driving to his apartment? The days were filled with more and more fun-filled moments of spontaneous enjoyment – things that never cost anything to enjoy but they both found so enjoyable. They began to enjoy being together more and more every day.

Pete Gallagher knew he was a fairly normal male and also knew his commitments to his values and Nanette's in that having any sexual encounters with this lovely lady would probably never happen. He also knew that getting closer and closer to her meant more and more cold showers. He wanted to marry her but knew he could never keep up with her, her way of life, or that his family would ever agree to such an arrangement. Yet, there was something about this lady that he just could not resist. He needed her in his life. Why did she hang around with him? What could he possibly offer her in return for what she was giving to him? He now had a reason to get up every day.

Nanette was growing more and more fond of Pete by the day. She knew she was not prepared to entertain the thoughts of a third marriage and marriage to this man would certainly be a challenge. She wasn't sure she could meet that challenge. She needed to know a lot more about brain injury, how it would affect her, and what a future with this man might include. She was also very afraid of getting close to another man. He seemed to like to drink and she was petrified that she was again attracted to a man who liked liquor. She already had two marriages to two alcoholic husbands; she couldn't be linked to another. What could he see in her? She now weighed 335 pounds. What could have attracted her to him? She was huge -- very overweight. She wondered if her weight would be an issue as time went on. How could she bring herself to deal with all the frustrations going on in her own mind? She was so elated to be sharing life with a man who seemed to care so much about her and scared at the same time. All Nanette needed to do, however, was think about Pete Gallagher's hugs and she would forget all her troubles for that moment. He was the gentlest and kindest man she had ever known. He touched her with such tenderness and caring, something Nanette Squires never knew with any man she ever dated or married. There was certainly something different about Pete Gallagher – she had to obtain more knowledge about what made this man tick!

It was only a few weeks after Nanette and Pete first began to see each other that the Community Church held their annual Strawberry Supper. Nanette was serving as a hostess to greet folks on their arrival and direct them where they needed to go. She was also acting as backup for the cashiers. Nanette agreed to take a break when Pete arrived to join him for dinner. She was standing in the lobby waiting for folks to arrive when she saw him walk across the parking lot with another woman. She had no idea who this other woman was but she knew she was very beautiful and they apparently knew one another because they were talking incessantly. Nanette was very nervous because she was apprehensive as to whom this other woman could be. Pete had not mentioned bringing someone with him. Perhaps he forgot he was meeting her and brought another date. Pete walked through the door and looked around for a minute before spotting Nanette.

"Hi, Nanette," said Pete. "I'd like you to meet my mother, Ellie Gallagher. Mom, this is Nanette Squires."

"Hello, Mrs. Gallagher. Welcome to our church. We are very glad you could come and enjoy our Strawberry Supper with us. Do you already have your tickets for the supper?" responded Nanette in a sigh of relief. Thank goodness she had put on a good dress and decent shoes. Never did she think she would meet Pete's mother this way. Surprised again; Pete was always full of them because he never remembered to tell her things before they happened.

"Well, it's nice to meet you too, Nanette," confused Ellie Gallagher responded. "No, I have reserved our tickets but need to pay for them."

"Will you be able to join us for supper, Nanette?" asked Pete.

"Yes, I can now. I have someone who can fill in for me," replied Nanette. I have reserved us some seats but I don't know if there are three there." As she looked over at the table she had reserved for her and Pete there were only two seats available, but one of the back tables had three. It would be a bit of a squeeze, but they could fit in there. "Follow me."

Both women were very confused. Ellie Gallagher knew something was up between her son, Pete and this lady who apparently appeared to be more than a friend. She seemed like a lovely person, but was concerned if she knew as much as she should before getting too involved with her son. What was she expecting from her son?

Nanette was stunned by the appearance of Pete's mother. She was twenty years younger than herself (there already was a large age difference between her and Pete – she being eight years older than Pete). She didn't look her age at all. She was so pretty, so put together, with a wonderful figure. With a mother like that, how could he have any attraction to her who was so overweight? Surely his mother noticed that also. She was very nervous throughout dinner. Then Pete did the unmentionable – he grabbed Nanette's hand and his mother's and made a comparison between how beautiful his mother's hands and nails were. Nanette quickly pulled her hands away. She worked hard for years, sometimes working as many as four jobs to make a living to support herself and her sons. Before that she had her hands in water much of the time while working at the bakery with Bart. Of course, her hands looked like a mess. Wonder what his mother did for a living to have such beautiful hands – everything about her was beautiful.

As the evening went on Nanette began to relax. As she did, she noticed how attentive Pete was to his mother. She was such a well-mannered lady and seemed so pleasant. She never once made mention of the fact that Nanette was so overweight – such a very sensitive subject for her. Nanette remembered how her parents had both told her to pay closer attention to how a man treats his mother before you get too involved with him. The way he treats his mother will probably be the way he will treat you. Well, if that was the case, Nanette knew from this one meeting she wouldn't have any trouble in this area of their relationship. Now Nanette knew why Pete had such a perfect looking apartment and wore some of the finest clothing. His mother cared deeply for her son and made sure his life was as good as she could make it. Nanette felt very much at ease with Ellie by the end of the evening.

Pete called Nanette one Tuesday evening to inform her of his support group meeting. "Hi, Nan." "I have a support group meeting with my TBI group tomorrow evening and my mother cannot go with me. Would you be interested in going?"

Nanette had not heard about this before and was at a loss for words. "What is a TBI support group?" asked Nanette.

"Oh a bunch of us who have had a traumatic brain injury get together at the college for a session with a doctor who has been doing a bunch of research on brain injury," replied Pete. She usually has a great program and you might learn more about brain injury.

Now Nanette was all ears. This is exactly what she needed. "Yeah, sure. I'll go with you. Can you pick me up at the house?"

"Will do!"

Nanette began to understand in vivid details more about Pete's brain injury. It terrified her and she was not sure she could handle this. She, however, continued to ask questions and gather information. Dr. Sarah

Rigley took Nanette aside after the video and meeting, and explained a lot more things to her. She also told her about the Traumatic Brain Injury Association and that they are in every state. She offered her lots of literature to help her get more acquainted with what TBI really was and how to deal with it.

In the following weeks, Nanette became involved in a second Support Group for TBI that Pete was also involved with that was sponsored by Easter Seals. In this group, there was a group meeting with a special guest speaker about a specific topic each time they met. These topics could include the reaction to a brain injured person driving in traffic, to how the brain itself functions and what happens when it is injured, to how the nervous system doesn't respond to hunger like folks without a TBI. Nanette took all this information in very short order and learned more about what Pete was going through than she ever imagined. With the help of Dr. Harkins, Dr. Rigley and the Easter Seals program she became more and more prepared to deal with a full-time relationship with Pete; she knew he was more than worth it. He had to be the kindest man she ever knew and he had fallen very much in love with her. She wondered if she should let herself feel love again but it was very hard not to love this loving man – he was the best thing that ever happened to her.

Nanette accompanied Pete to several of his meetings with Dr. Harkins whom continued to see Pete on a monthly basis. It was an eye-opener for Pete during one of these sessions.

"Pete, you have to listen very closely to me," said Dr. Harkins. Nanette is a steam locomotive engine. You are the caboose. Don't ever try keeping up with her. You will never be able to. When you can accept that she has the power to charge full steam ahead, you'll be ready to accept a good relationship with this wonderful woman. This is a strange meeting of the minds, but I suspect she has what it takes to get you both balanced into a good life."

Pete left that session almost on top of the world. He was very comfortable knowing that Nanette had the power to keep them going – he had let others help him through life. He would just have to learn to let this woman do that for him too, if he wanted her in his life – and he did. How would he feel like a man if he could not protect her and take care of her like his father had taken care of his mother all these years?

After several other group meetings, Pete and Nanette met Dr. Rigley again after the meeting. She asked to see them privately.

"I know you two are getting more and more serious every day," said Dr. Rigley. "If the two of you really want a relationship to work between you, I strongly suggest you begin to see, a psychologist that specializes in brain injury. You both have a lot of baggage coming into this relationship and you both need to be aware of what you have ahead of you. I have a list of names I can give you."

Within the next weeks, Nanette and Pete began to see Dr. Robert Cutler. He was not particularly a specialist for brain injury but his wife was. He did specialize in couple's counseling. With their permission, he would talk over their case from time to time with his wife, and agreed to take them on as new patients. They agreed and began weekly visits with Dr. Cutler who provided them many, many new insights into what they had been through individually, together, and what they might encounter as a couple in the future. These sessions continued for two solid years.

Nanette began to feel closer and closer to Pete every day and now felt very armed with a ton of resources and information about what Pete felt. Pete on the other hand had to deal with what Nanette had been though in two very rough marriages to two alcoholic husbands who abused her physiologically and physically. Pete was nowhere near accepting these things as Nanette. It would take months working with Dr. Cutler to iron out those feelings for Pete. He still could not understand what Nanette saw in him as a physically challenged person with short-term memory problems and a personality that sometimes was just not him. That second personality Pete and Nanette began to nickname as "Pete II".

One evening at Nanette's house, Pete began to talk to Nanette about something she had already told him about several times. In frustration, she raised her voice and Pete II came out in full bloom. She had seen this before, but this time it scared her. She wasn't sure what to do, but spoke frankly to Pete.

"Pete, I don't like what you're saying or doing," said Nanette in a sharp and harsh voice.

"Then sing along with me, honey!"

"Pete, this is serious. You need to pay attention to what you are doing."

Pete waved his hands freely everywhere and began dancing around the kitchen singing something that sounded like baby gibberish. Nanette was not sure what to do.

She took Pete by the hand and sat him at the kitchen table.

"Pete, stop acting like this. We need to have some dinner and then you need to get some sleep. You can sleep on my sofa," she said in a very soft voice.

"Ok," said Pete acting very much like he was drunk.

Nanette served dinner quickly and then put Pete to bed on her sofa. She was afraid to let him drive home this way. Anyway, the next day was Saturday and perhaps he would be better with a good night's sleep.

The next day Pete was himself and he and Nanette were able to talk about the events of the night before. They were also able to discuss these events with Dr. Cutler who let them know that when Pete II came out was probably because Pete did not get enough sleep and when Nanette raised her voice, it totally disconnected him from himself. That would be the only way to deal with his surroundings. Nanette had to learn patience – that became the biggest word in her vocabulary over the next several months – patience, patience, and more patience.

After about three and a half months, enjoying each other tremendously, lots of research, attending two support groups every month and seeing Dr. Cutler every week, Pete and Nanette were growing closer and closer every day. It was after church one Sunday, when Nanette joined Pete at his apartment. She was sitting at his table as he was putting things away.

"You know I think that April is a good time of the year to get married," said Pete just as nonchalant as possible.

"No, I think June is better; the weather is better in New England," replied Nanette again just as nonchalant as he had.

Pete took out a calendar and they both looked at the calendar for the year after next – more than eighteen months away.

"Oh, look, Pete," exclaimed Nanette. "May 8th is on a Saturday. That's a perfect day since Jake and Jamie were born on the 8th of the month. It must be a lucky day."

"Then May 8, 1999 it is," replied Pete as he turned to do his dishes that he left from the morning.

Nanette got up, a little perplexed by what had just happened and said, "You never proposed to me. Was that supposed to be a proposal?"

"Oh, yeah," said Pete. "Would you marry me?" Peter's hands were up to his elbows in soap as he leaned over to Nanette.

Nanette began to laugh so hard and looked at him with such loving eyes, "Yes, Pete Gallagher, I will marry you on May 8, 1999. That was some proposal!"

One of Pete Gallagher's lifetime dreams was coming true! He was getting married.

Chapter XIII

The Aftermath and Fallout of the Proposal

Now that Pete and Nanette made a commitment to one another in accepting each other through Pete's marriage proposal, they were faced with what this would mean to everyone around them, their families, their friends, Pete's doctors, the AILA Program and their future together. It was more than Nanette could comprehend all at once. So it had to be broken down in small pieces.

That evening at Nanette's house while she was making dinner, Pete picked up the phone to call his mother and tell her the good news.

"Hi, Mom," greeted Pete.

"Hi, Pete. How are you?" responded his mother.

"I'm on top of the world. Nanette and I are going to get married."

"Oh, really. When Pete? Have you two set a date?"

"Yeah, in May," replied Pete.

"Oh my," Ellie responded in utter disbelief. Did this young woman know what she is getting into? To get married in only a few months.

"Would you like to talk to Nanette?" responded Pete.

"Well, yes I would!"

"Hello Mrs. Gallagher," answered Nanette.

"Well, you two have some news," replied Ellie. "How exciting! Pete tells me you are planning to get married in May. We sure have a lot of work to do before then, a lot of work to do!" Ellie hoped the panic in her voice didn't come across in a negative manner to Nanette.

"Yes, I know but we have time, lots of time," responded Nanette. Pete wants to have a traditional wedding and that is going to take some real planning to pull that off with a lot of details to work out.

"You don't really have that much time if you plan to be married in May."

"Sure we do. We are not being married until a year from this May and it is only September now. We have more than a year and a half to prepare and plan for all sorts of things," responded Nanette.

"Oh, not for another year," Ellie let out a gasp of air that Nanette could feel through the phone.

"Sorry, Mrs. Gallagher," replied Nanette. "I sure didn't mean for you to panic. I realize there are a lot of issues to work out and that Pete and I have a lot of planning and talking to get through everything as well as to consult with lots of doctors, counselors, and family before an actual wedding can be held. I want to take our time and do this right."

"That's good," answered Ellie. "Sounds like you have things under control. Good for you. You and Pete will have to come over for dinner one night real soon."

"That is very nice of you. We'd be happy to join you for dinner," responded Nanette.

Ellie Gallagher got off the phone and sat for several moments before she could compose herself. Pete was going to get married. She thought this was never going to happen and she was watching her brain-injured son planning a marriage. Composure was difficult but as Ellie began thinking more and more about what Nanette said, it sounded as though she was prepared to go through a lot of preparations. She had to be someone very special to take on this challenge. Ellie needed to gather the family to make plans for Pete's new life and what that was going to mean for everyone.

"Well, we have one family member who's been told," said Pete. "You know my brothers and sister will know very soon from this one call. Now we have to let your family know."

"I will be seeing Jake this weekend and I'll tell him," responded Nanette. After I do that, I will have to call Jamie now that he is living in Washington, DC and let him know."

Nanette and Pete continued to see Dr. Cutler and discuss not only their relationship, but also their plans for the future.

"Dr. Cutler, Nanette has accepted my marriage proposal and we are going to be married a year from May," said Pete in their next session.

"Well, congratulations, you two," responded Dr. Cutler in genuine compassion and acceptance. "You know we will need to work through a lot of issues and how you plan to deal with all of them, but for now, let's just focus on what is of importance right now."

"What do you mean, Dr. Cutler?" Nanette questioned.

"Well, first how do the two of you feel about making such a commitment to one another?"

"I feel great," said Pete

"Me too," said Nanette

"That's great, but have you thought about where you will live, how you will pay for your everyday living expenses, and medical insurance?" responded Dr. Cutler.

"Sure, Pete will move into my house," replied Nanette. "It is certainly big enough for both of us and should provide us with more than enough room. I have two jobs and make a good living. I am supporting the house now on my own, can't see how that could be a lot different, and I carry very adequate medical insurance coverage through my employer."

"Besides, Dr. Cutler, I have my Social Security disability checks every month. I can contribute to Nanette's expenses of the house, and I am working a part-time job. We should be fine. I have medical insurance through the insurance company my father worked at," Pete uttered all in one large breath. He was hopeful that Dr. Cutler wasn't taking the place of his father and trying to discourage them from getting married, something he wanted more than anything in the entire world.

"You have some great plans, but let's break them down and think about this one by one," said Dr. Cutler. "Pete, you will lose your housing subsidy as soon as you marry. Are you aware of that? Also, you will probably lose the medical insurance that was provided by your father before his death. Nanette will have to add you to hers, not a problem, I am sure, but you need to make sure it will be sufficient to cover the expenses you have and those that might occur in the future. I think you have some great plans as long as you both are aware and accept what you will lose when you marry as much as you will gain when you marry."

All of these things were more than Pete had thought about and now was more concerned than ever if he should put Nanette through all this. It took months and months of discussions with Dr. Cutler for them to work through these issues and decide that marriage was the "*right*" thing for the both of them. They met in church, were both raised in church, and living together was out of the question. Nanette felt she was caught in a web of church and state; where was that separation the government always talked about. If she married Pete, they stood to lose a lot of financial help, yet if she didn't marry him and they just lived together, they would be living a life of sin in the eyes of God; not an option for either of them.

"Pete, don't think about everything that Dr. Cutler just told us," said Nanette. Neither one of us can possibly conceive all these ideas and make plans for all of these issues in one night. It is going to take a lot of time and time is on our side. Let's just take one day at a time and in the process continue to enjoy each other's company."

"It's just so much. How can getting married be so complicated?" retorted Pete.

"Marriage itself is not something to enter into lightly, Pete," responded Nanette. It is very complicated planning a wedding without all the other issues we already bring to this relationship. You have not begun to deal with all of what I have been through. We have been focusing on your brain injury and how I would deal with that. I need to know you understand my background before we can move too far forward. It will take time, Pete, and time is what we have, lots of time. We are in no rush. We have each other, we love each other, and God has brought us together, so we just have to let God lead us through these times."

"Nanette, you're right. I know that God brought us together and you're right, he has a plan for us and we just need to let go and let God get us there. Thanks for the reminder!"

Jake came by the house that Saturday to pick up some boxes of things he had stored there.

"Hi, Mom," Jake greeted his mother with a big smile and hug as he entered her door. "Want to go get some lunch while I'm here? My treat!"

"You're on," responded Nanette. "Let's get your boxes first and then we can go get some lunch together."

Nanette was so nervous to tell Jake about her plans to marry Pete. They gathered up the five or six boxes Jake came to get and headed out to the restaurant. They carried on a general conversation over lunch, catching up on what was going on in each other's lives, but Nanette skirted the issue of her upcoming marriage. As Jake was driving his mother back to her house after lunch, Nanette decided was the time.

"Jake, I have to tell you something and I'm not quite sure how you will take it," said Nanette.

"What is it Mom?" questioned Jake. "Are you sick with something? Are you okay?"

"No, no, nothing like that," responded Nanette. "Jake, I have accepted a marriage proposal from Pete. I know, he will be my third husband and yeah, that does scare me a lot, but he is such a nice man. He is so good to me and he truly does love me."

"Mom, that's great!" exclaimed Jake. "Hey, you've been down some tough roads and lived a junky life. I don't think you'd take up company, much less get married, to another jerk. I'm sure he's a great guy Mom. I'm sure we will all think he is just as wonderful as you say he is."

"Oh, Jake," gasped Nanette. "It is so good to hear you say that. You know Grandma and Grandpa are going to have a fit. I've been divorced from Bart for more than eight years now and I don't think they ever wanted to see me get married again knowing my track record."

"Don't worry about it, Mom," answered Jake. "They too will accept him. Just give them some time to get used to the idea. You say he is physically challenged?"

"Yes, but unless you see him walk or spent a lot of time with him, you'd hardly know it," answered Nanette. "He has short-term memory loss and that's probably his greatest difficulty. So he probably won't remember your name for months after he is first introduced to you. Once it is four or five months stored into his brain, he will suddenly be able to remember it just fine."

"Mom, I think you'll be fine. Sounds like you have found yourself someone who really makes you very happy. For that, I am very glad and I wish you the very best forever," replied Jake. "Remember, Mom, I love you and I only want whoever lives with you to love you too!"

Jake only met Pete once before but worked with Lee and Pete to help remove shrubs from Nanette's new home. He thought he was a decent enough fellow and if he made his mother happy, then what business was it of his that he should point fingers. She'd been through enough in her life and successfully raised her three sons sacrificing more than most for their wellbeing. He was very happy for his mother that she wouldn't have to be alone anymore. He liked Pete for the amount of time he had spent with him.

Nanette and Pete were well aware of the issues they were about to face as they broke the news to more and more people, but probably not as prepared to address all the issues.

"Pete, we have to stay positive about our decision to marry," said Nanette.

"I know, but just how are we going to handle the negative comments every time someone in the family tells us all the bad things that "*are*" going to happen particularly when we don't know whether they will or not."

"Exactly, Pete, and neither do any of the members of our families! We have to remain positive that together we will make a difference in each other lives. You make a huge difference in my life. You are the first man since I was a little girl under the protective arms of my father that has really cared about me and really shown me true love. That is more than I could ever imagine. Just the way you touch me makes me know I am safe and that you are there for me. You make a difference for me, Pete, a real difference. That's what we remember when we face the negative comments – how much we love each other and care about our future together."

"That's what I love so much about you," said Pete. "You have such a sensible head on your shoulders. I want to make a difference for you and sometimes I think I have to just be extra baggage for you – another problem for you to "*solve*" and that's the last thing I want to be. You know you are everything to me; I love you so much and you have opened a whole new life for me. The last thing I would ever want is to be a burden."

"You're not a burden, Pete. I love who you are and the person you are. What might look like a burden to someone else, is really a personal thank you for providing so much to me. When someone cares for another person, they want to go out of their way to do what they can to make life easier and more fulfilling for that loved one. That's how I feel about you."

"Just how did I get so lucky to meet such a wonderful person as you? You are the light of my life! I really do love you, Nanette!"

Labor Day was fast approaching and it was the annual Gallagher family reunion when everyone in the family gathered at the shore for a weekend of fun and catching up on everyone's lives. Pete asked Nanette to join him for that long weekend. She agreed with the understanding she would get her own place to stay making it a bit less awkward for his family. Pete agreed but also knew he wasn't about to let her out of his sight for any long periods of time. This would be the first time Nanette would get a chance to meet the entire family. She had only met Pete's mother up to this point.

Pete and Nanette drove to the beach house that Friday evening after checking her into her motel. Nanette meet two of Pete's nieces for the first time and was just delighted to be in their presence. They were so much like him. They were open to her and never made a negative comment about her weight or the fact that she was spending time with their uncle.

As the evening grew, more and more family came. There were two brothers and one sister with their spouses. Seven nieces and nephews and Pete's mother. When Pete's youngest brother Billy came through the door and before Pete could utter a sound, Billy place his four-month old baby girl in this strange woman's arms. To Nanette's delight the baby took to her and in no time was fast asleep where she remained for hours. The room was filled to capacity as everyone enjoying cocktails and hors d'oveuvres. Pete was the first to speak after all the introductions were made.

"Hey guys, I want to tell you guys something," Pete said in a very abrupt voice making everyone stop talking instantly and turn towards Pete. He was nervous but knew the spotlight was on him now. Nanette sat in silence and held her breath while Pete began.

"You all have met Nanette. Well, in case you didn't know, she and I have known each other through our church for some time, actually several years now. We began dating or seeing each other a few months ago.

Nanette and I are planning on getting married in May of 1999 – more than a year and a half away!"

Ellie Gallagher suspected Pete would announce their marriage plans but was stunned when she actually heard it. Pete seemed serious about this and now what was she supposed to do? If only her husband was here, he would know what to do. She was silent as she listened to the reactions of the rest of the family.

"Hey, old fellow!" exclaimed Billy Gallagher, Pete's younger brother. "That's great news. Congratulations, and to you too, Nanette. I sure hope you know what you're getting into with this young man! He can be a handful you know."

"Thanks, Billy," replied Nanette. "I'm well aware of the handful he can be, but when you feel the way I do about your brother, it is all well worth it. I know I have lots to learn, but I am a very willing participant."

Stanley Gallagher stood by as he listened to the exchange between his brothers. He wasn't so sure he had the same feelings right now about this marriage thing that his younger brother did. Pete had several girl friends over the years and many of them he thought he should marry. However, he never brought one to the reunion and announced wedding plans. This was certainly something a bit different.

"Well, old boy – you think you're up for marriage, huh!" proclaimed Stanley patting Pete on the back. "It's not all a bed of roses you know. It can be rather strenuous and I'm sure we'll have to have lots of discussion here before you two can proceed with these plans. This is not the usual set of circumstances and you stand to lose a lot Pete."

"I won't lose anything Stan," said Pete. "I will gain a beautiful wife, a partner, and three great sons. Someone who makes me very happy and someone I want to spend the rest of my life being with."

"Stan, I understand your concern and I can assure you I will make it my life's mission to take care of Pete the best way I know possible," responded Nanette.

"Well, we'll have to see about that," replied Stan.

"I think dinner is ready. Let's all gather on the deck for a fine meal," interrupted Ellie Gallagher.

Pete looked at Nanette and knew she was taken back by the comments that were been made, but they both remained composed and continued to enjoy a relaxing weekend. Nanette got a chance to get to know all of Pete's family and had a wonderful weekend with everyone, but felt that Stan was a bit more reserved as though she was now a threat to him in some way. She decided before the weekend was over that he was just being a protective brother to his physically challenged older brother whom he adored and wanted only the very best for him. Of course, she was an intrusion into the family structure and how things had been run for the last several years; keeping Pete safe, comfortable and well provided for were his main concern. Nanette knew her presence into the family was going to put everyone in an upheaval again, and no one really wanted to deal with that. It was going to be a few challenging months ahead.

The long weekend had proved to be successful for the most part and now Nanette and Pete faced yet another tense moment in telling her parents.

"Let's invite your parents to dinner," said Pete. "We can tell them then."

"That's sounds okay," replied Nanette. "I'll call them right now."

Nanette made the phone call only to be asked by Lee to join him and Ann to a trip north to see the foliage and to have a famous "pancake and maple syrup" lunch at their favorite maple-sugar farm. Pete and Nanette agreed and joined Lee and Ann the following Saturday for the excursion north. The four-some enjoyed wonderful conversation all the way to their "favorite" restaurant while enjoying the sites. After enjoying their meal, Pete thought the time was right.

"Nanette and I would like to share something with the both of you," said Pete

"What's that?" responded Lee Peters

"We have decided to get married in May of 1999 – about a year and a half from now," Pete quickly got the details out.

"Well, that's wonderful! "I only hope you two decide to get to know each other before taking the plunge again Nanette. You two are planning on living together first aren't you?" replied the 82-year old Ann Peters.

"Mother, how could you!" exclaimed Nanette. "Of course, we'll get to know each other more and more every day, however, Pete and I met in the church and we have moral issues with living together."

"Now, Ann let's just be excited for the kids, and not get into their personal lives," interjected Lee. It's none of our business how they decide to do this. We just need to support their decision and be there when they need us."

"Okay, okay," replied Ann. "I just don't want you to make another mistake, Nanette."

"I understand, Mom," replied Nanette. Just let me go through getting to know as much as I can about Pete and as Dad said, just support us as we make this big decision.

All in all, Nanette and Pete thought it went better than expected even though neither one of them expected the response they got from Ann Peters. Most of the family now knew and throughout all this, Nanette and Pete continued to have their counseling sessions with Dr. Cutler. As the family encounters kept bringing up more and more issues, Dr. Cutler was kept up to speed with the reactions.

"I know the two of you have met in the church and have shared a good deal of Christian life together bringing your values and moral ideals into each other's lives," said Dr. Cutler. "That seems to be a very large common bond between the two of you. However, you are already beginning to deal with the family issues and the issue surrounding a fairly large wedding. There will be the new issue of moving Pete into your house, Nanette, and a new neighborhood. That will introduce more new things to Pete constantly. If you introduce new major changes to Pete quickly, you may trigger more problems for him than you are prepared to handle. He might not be able to handle all the confusion of planning a large wedding, a honeymoon, moving, and then moving into a new neighborhood much less learning how to live with a new wife. My recommendation would be for you to both think about Pete moving now into your house, Nanette before you get married. I know that's not what you intended to do, but it makes sense in order to keep Pete running all his mental facility smoothly."

"Oh my!" gasped Nanette. "No, that's not what we planned to do at all. That would be living in sin. We can't do that. I know I've been married before, but I am not a person that just pops guys in and out of my house on a whim, Dr. Cutler."

"It's okay, honey," Pete tried to smooth out the conversation before Nanette got too caught up in it. "Let's just try to think about this calmly."

"That's all I ask," said Dr. Cutler. Just think about the possibilities. "It might prevent a lot of problems for the both of you going through so many changes."

The next several weeks held many conversations about Pete moving into Nanette's new house. Nanette didn't have a problem with Pete moving in, but did have a problem doing so before they were married. This was a major problem for both of them.

"I have an idea, Nanette," said Pete one evening while she was preparing dinner. "Why don't we just have our own little wedding together now?"

"How can we do that?" replied Nanette. "It wouldn't be legal if we did that."

"We don't have to have it legal, we only need to make a commitment to each other between each other and in the eyes of God," responded Pete.

"You mean no marriage license with the government, but instead a bible between us as we say our vows to each other?" exclaimed Nanette now more excited about this possibility than ever before.

"Yeah!" said Pete. "We can do it right now."

"No!" replied Nanette. "This has to be meaningful or it just isn't right. Let's take a trip to the ocean. There is a great spot in Maine I know about and it would be perfect. We can stand on the mountain overlooking the ocean and say our vows to each other there.

"Sounds perfect to me, honey!" said Pete. "This weekend then?"

Nanette and Pete took a drive for three and a half hour to Maine to unite themselves in their own commitment to one another before God. While they were there for their short stay, they took walks along the shore on the Marginal way and down to the cove. They ate at wonderful restaurants, the three meals they squeezed in. The both love lobster so they were sure to have a lobster dinner before having to return home. They were even able to fit in a lobster boat trip where they watch the owners capture lobsters, measure them and decide if they were big enough to keep.

As the sun was setting they decided to take another walk along the Marginal Way. It was a breathtaking moment for the both of them as they stood on the mountain overlooking the Atlantic Ocean and listening to the waves beat against the rocks. It was almost nightfall when they climbed to the top and the sun was setting making the most spectacular backdrop for the new bride and groom. They committed themselves to one another before God and knew from that moment on they would be bonded together for life – for their lives together. It made both of them feel better knowing they had committed to each other before God whether there was a wedding or not. If they moved in together as they thought they might, they could do so knowing they had made their commitment to each other in the eyes of God overlooking the Atlantic Ocean on a beautiful starry night as the sun set.

Teddy had been delighted with the news that Pete and Nanette were going to get married. As excited as he was, however, he hadn't expected pushing his mother to have Pete for dinner would lead to a marriage between them. Just how was his mother going to deal with all his physical and mental issues? Was she really up for the challenge? She had already endured so many issues in her life – what was this new endeavor and permanent adventure going to have in store for her?

"Mom, just be careful about what you're about to encounter," said Teddy. "Taking on a husband with so many needs might be more than you can handle."

"I know Teddy," responded Nanette. "It will be a challenge but I have attended two of Pete's support groups with him and have become acquainted with the doctors, specialists and a host of support people who are familiar with brain injury. They have begun to prepare me as to what I might expect as Pete ages, and although it is a scary thing to face, I would rather take my chances with someone who truly loves me and is good to me. I do love this man very much. Some of these folks in this field have researched brain injury and have encountered new developments every day. They pass on new information to us every month. Don't worry about me, Teddy; I'm a strong woman and I'm up for the challenge!"

"I hope so, Mom. I don't want you to have to go through any other negative things in your life. You've been through enough."

Pete was patiently waiting to talk to Teddy and kept trying to get Nanette to end her conversation with him so he could talk to Teddy over the phone.

"Hey, Teddy!" exclaimed Pete. "So you heard the news? Pretty exciting stuff, don't you think!"

"Yeah, Pete," responded Teddy a little apprehensive about this conversation with Pete. "So when is the big day going to happen?"

"Not until a year from May," explained Pete. We want to take our time and make sure everything is prepared correctly. There are a lot of deals to work out, not just the wedding, but all the living arrangements, finances and you know all the details of putting two lives together."

"Sounds like you two are trying to work the details out," commented Teddy.

"We are," said Pete. "Listen, Teddy, since you are a jeweler, do you think we might be able to get a deal on a diamond ring for Nanette? I want her to have something special, because she is special."

"Yeah, sure, just come in to the store Saturday morning and we'll look at what I can do," replied Teddy.

"Thanks, Teddy. This means so much to me, you'll never know! We'll be in Saturday and thanks again." Pete hung up the phone and glanced at Nanette who had been listening to his call.

"You don't have to do this," exclaimed Nanette.

"Oh, yes I do," proclaimed Pete. I've never been married before and I want the very best I can afford for you. You know that won't be much, but I'd buy you the moon if I could."

"You know, Pete, I have one of my old diamonds that doesn't mean much to me as far as sentiment is concerned and we could probably trade it in and get something that would be wonderful," explained Nanette.

"Are you sure you wouldn't mind doing that?" questioned Pete.

"Not at all, it would be great to get that out of the house," replied Nanette. "Out with the old and in with the new; I need to move it out and get on with our lives."

Pete was without words for the first time in a long while. He knew the diamond she was referring to and knew it would produce a sizeable amount of money on a trade-in. This was going to mean that he could afford to buy her a much bigger and nicer engagement ring. He was very excited about how everything was falling into place.

On Saturday they met Teddy in his store and picked out a beautiful diamond ring using Nanette's trade-in value to afford the new ring. There was still a small balance but Pete felt it was manageable. Teddy would have the ring ready the early part of the next week just in time for their planned trip through Virginia and into West Virginia. They planned to end up in Washington, DC to visit with Jamie and Candice who were now living there. This would be so special.

Pete and Nanette began to pack their bags for their first motor trip some eight to ten hours away. It would be a challenge to drive that long and Nanette wasn't sure how much of the driving Pete would be up to. They loaded the car on Friday evening so they could pack a cooler in the morning and head out early. This would be a fun trip and ending up seeing Jamie and Candice would be the icing on the cake. Nanette wasn't sure how Jamie would take the news about their upcoming marriage. She feared that Jamie would be the one child of hers who would object the loudest and be a bit skeptical about Pete. He was the child who seemed more suspicious about change than the other two. Time would tell and she wouldn't worry about that part of their trip until they got there.

The trip was long. Longer than it should have been. They stopped frequently to use rest rooms and get a drink or food to eat. Pete needed to stretch his legs often and that slowed them down more than Nanette had counted on. During the slow trip they were able to see some scenery which was beautiful but their focus was on highway driving and the urge to arrive before sunset at their appointed motel in West Virginia. However, try as they might they didn't arrive at their motel until just after sundown. In spite of their delays, most of their driving time had been in daylight. Pete was able to drive about a half hour or so every other time they stopped which gave Nanette time to recover before she would pick up the driving again. They were very tired and turned in early once they arrived in Virginia – the next day they would look around at all the highlights of the area and get to enjoy an area neither of them had visited before.

Upon waking in the morning, getting that first cup of coffee and tea, the couple headed for their patio and basked in the beautiful sunshine and lush green surrounding. They left Connecticut in brisk fall temperature where trees had already turned color and now only a few miles south relatively speaking, here were beautiful rolling hills in the vivid color of green with trees standing tall as though summer had taken a longer than usual spell at showing itself. Nanette and Pete lazed around in the sunshine for more than two hours catching up on some rest while they enjoyed their beverages and breakfast. They decided to visit a museum and walked through a local park for their day's activities.

They drove to the museum and enjoyed some archeological artifacts that neither of them remembered witnessing such a display before. This appeared to be an area that left many remains of various species of animals and humans, which the museum captured and showed wonderful displays of what probably appeared here many thousands of years earlier. Pete enjoyed the displays but got a bit impatient walking the entire museum and they left before lunch. They stopped at a local diner and had a sandwich before taking in the park. Nanette knew that Pete probably wouldn't hold up to walking very far in the park but it would be an experience to see the natural landscape and seeing some of the park would be better than not seeing it at all.

They walked further than Nanette had expected and the scenery was just magnificent. They both enjoyed being outdoors in the sunshine and witnessing the landscape in its entirety without any fall colors yet appearing. The various colors of green brought so much to the rolling hills and vivid shrubs and flowering plants. Since Pete had a love of outdoors, this experience seemed to waken his senses far more than the stuffy confines of the indoor museum.

They saw a theatrical theatre on their way back to the motel and decided that would be a fun thing to look into for the following evening. The plan for tonight was to relax with a box supper in front of the television and rest up for another day of adventure tomorrow.

The following day Nanette and Pete made their plans for how they would spend their last full day in West Virginia and how their motor trip would continue the next day before taking them back through Washington. They decided to take in the sights of the quaint little town with all its shops to see what might be interesting. The evening was booked with tickets to a play and dinner at the "French" restaurant next door. Pete couldn't remember if he had ever been to a French restaurant before but was game to give it a try. He had an appetite that was every woman's dream – just feed him no matter what it was. He most likely would like it. Perfect for Nanette because she had a fetish for cooking and as Pete called it, "creating in the kitchen".

They returned from their shopping with few bags of loot, as they didn't see a whole lot that interested them enough to warrant stuffing their luggage further. They dressed for dinner and drove to the restaurant, which was within two doors of the theater. Nanette was enjoying every morsel of her meal when she realized Pete was savoring this new cuisine probably for the first time or that he was not accustomed to eating this way often and wanted the experience to last. Either way she thought he was funny as every bite lasted longer than the last one and it pleased her that she had picked such a fine restaurant for one of their first trips together. This would be a pleasant memory to last them a lifetime.

After dinner they entered the theater and were excited to see a play together. It didn't take Nanette long to realize that Pete was having a lot of difficulty remembering the characters in the play. She was constantly telling him who was who and who did what. However, by intermission and a little catch up, the second half seemed to connect better for him and he truly seemed to have enjoyed a delightful evening together.

They held hands as they left the theater and walked to their car. Nanette caught her heals in the sidewalk as they were walking and realizing she was holding Pete's hand, knew he would fall as soon as she did. She twisted her arm and flew Pete across in front of her where he landed on a thick grassy area. He appeared to get up from his fall with no problems, but Nanette had a large wound on her leg from knee to ankle with lots of cuts and bruising was sure to arise. Nanette had difficulty getting up and walking, so Pete helped her up and she limped back to the car where they had some tissue. He hurried her back to the motel where he very tentatively washed her wound, found some ice and made a homemade ice bag for her.

He called to the front desk and got some antiseptic and bandages to cover her wounds where he could. Nanette soon recognized the attention Pete was giving her – something she had never received before since she was a child and living with her parents. This was refreshing and one more credit to Pete for the wonderful husband he was going to be.

Leg bandaged and bags packed the following morning the couple headed for the Shenandoah National Park. This park has a motor trail that runs the length of the Appalachian Mountains but they decided to drive just 20 miles along the scenic route and stop at various lookouts to catch the exquisite views, taking pictures as they went along. They followed their planned course of action and drove to the Laverne Caverns on their route to Washington. They stopped on the green and enjoyed their picnic lunch Nanette had prepared in front of a tall tower which played chimes every hour on the hour. After lunch they crossed the street and entered the caverns, a feat that Nanette wasn't sure if Pete would be able to walk through with all the twists and turns, stairs and ramps leading down to the caverns. He amazed her once again. If she could do this, then so could he. He was experiencing some new adventures with the "love of his life" and he wasn't about to miss a thing – he wanted to be as normal as possible and enjoy as many moments with her as he could. This was another one of those moments the couple would remember for their lifetime.

They were now only a few hours from Jamie and Candice on their visit to Washington, DC. Nanette was anxious to see Jamie as it had been a while since their last visit, but she also knew he would be the son with more apprehension about her upcoming marriage to Pete than the other two. They arrived at Jamie's apartment just before dinner.

"Hey, Mom!" yelled Jamie excited to be seeing his Mom. "Great to see you, and this must be Pete."

"Good to see you too, son," replied Nanette. "And yes this is Pete Gallagher, your soon to be step-father."

"Good to meet you," Jamie retorted as he jumped in an obvious two-steps backward. The apparent news of their engagement had not reached Jamie and he was abruptly taken back literally by the news. "Oh, so you two have decided to get *married*?" questioned Jamie.

"Yes, we have, Jamie," interjected Pete. "We are planning a wedding for a year from May. In the meantime, not only do we have a lot of details to work out for the wedding, but we have decided to move in together."

This was more than Jamie was prepared to handle. "Come inside and meet Candice," Jamie replied changing the subject for a moment while he wrapped his head around the idea that his mother was about to enter a third marriage and this time to a "handicapped" man – was she insane?

"Hi, Candice," said Nanette giving her a big hug. "It's been so long since we had a chance to see you two and I'm glad we got a chance to make this trip. "Your apartment is lovely."

"Yes, it has been a long time. I'm so glad both of you could come for a visit. Oh come, see the view from the living room," responded Candice. "That is the Pentagon you're looking at."

"What a great place to live," said Pete. "It must be so great to see all the nation's landmarks and get to enjoy so much history."

"Oh it is," said Candice.

"So, have you heard or will this be as much a shock to you as it was to Jamie – Pete and I are getting married a year from May," invoked Nanette as she held out her hand to Candice for her to see her new engagement ring.

"Oh, wow," responded Candice. "You and my Mom are not wasting any time. She has met a man also and they are getting married this October."

"Time is ticking by, Candice," Nanette countered. "When you get to be our age, there is no time to waste. You either know right away that this is something to hang on to or you let it go quickly. I certainly had many chances I didn't want to take to first base. There was something different about Pete that makes me want to see second and third and run them all – straight to home plate. I am learning more and more about Pete every day and I like what I am uncovering, a lot! This guy is worth hanging on to, Candice."

"Then I wish you and Pete a lifetime of happiness," responded Candice.

Jamie took in all the conversation between his mother and Candice but had lots of reservations about what his mother thought she was uncovering. He was afraid taking care of someone with so many special needs would get old soon and his mother would run away from the entire situation. He was skeptical at the very least that this relationship would last until the planned wedding date.

The four-some went out for dinner as planned if they arrived on time. They enjoyed light conversation over dinner and Jamie didn't want to discuss their future plans in any detail while trying to eat. He thought it might give him a sore stomach and he frankly wasn't prepared for all this news. He was having a tough time trying to understand this relationship between his mother and Pete.

In the morning, Pete and Nanette joined Jamie at the local coffee shop while Candice chose to remain back at the apartment. When Pete strolled outside for a walk, Jamie took the opportunity to talk to his mother alone.

"Mom, do you really know what you are getting into?" demanded Jamie. This is going to take a lot of work on your part to keep him in balance mentally, much less keep his physical being functioning. This is taking on a lot of responsibility at your age. Are you sure this is what you want?"

"Don't worry so much, Jamie," Nanette replied getting a little fidgety about all the doubts. "I am working very hard with lots of doctors, specialists, and Pete and I are seeing a "couple's counselor" who has some background in brain injury. What Dr. Cutler doesn't understand, he consults with his wife who does have extensive background with brain injury. Yes, it is a learning curve and I have a lot to learn. I am a natural caregiver and if Pete needs someone to help him through life, why not me? I have never had a man in my life that has treated me so good, Jamie. He is kind, tender, and just the way he touches me tells me how much he truly loves me. I didn't know a man could really care so deeply for me the way Pete does. This is a wonderful experience for me, too. I think it is time I truly saw what a real relationship with a "man" was about and Pete is every bit a real "man!" Please don't be worried, Jamie. I do have things under control. Just to rest your mind, I'll promise you before Pete moves in, that if I think for one instant that I can get through the rest of my life with this man, I will break the relationship off, but I can assure you right now, that is not going to happen."

"Mom, I sure hope you're right," replied Jamie. "I just don't want to see you making another mistake. It has cost you dearly both emotionally and financially going through your last two mistakes. Please be careful and think hard before you get too far in over your head."

"It's okay, Jamie," replied Nanette. "He makes me laugh and enjoy life like I never have and that's a great feeling. We'll be just fine. It will take a lot of planning, but Pete and I will be just fine, you just wait and see."

For the most part their trip was a success although Nanette felt a bit drained trying to convince her second son that this marriage to Pete was the right thing for her to do. She left the following day for their long trip home not knowing for sure she had truly been successful in convincing Jamie of anything. He seemed to be the one that always questioned everything from the time he was a small child. Hopefully, perhaps as time moved along and he had more and more chance to get to know Pete better, he would understand his mother's relationship and what she truly saw in this wonderful man she had decided to marry.

It was October and the holidays would be approaching fast. Nanette thought rather than worry any more about what each member of both sides of the families thought about her marriage to Pete, she should focus her thoughts on getting ready for Thanksgiving and Christmas – the holidays always meant so much to her. After the holidays there would be enough time to think about the preparations for moving Pete into her home. That would take an act of God to help her work through all the paperwork, agencies, and financial responsibilities to make it work right for Pete. Was she up for this? Was Jamie right? Of course, she was up to this – this was "love" she had never experienced before and she knew that God had put her in Pete's life for a reason and Pete in her life for a reason – they were good for each other and they truly needed one another. They knew what the other one was thinking before it was ever said. How could this possibly be wrong – they had their Lord on their side and they both knew it!

Chapter XIV

The Vast Details and Preparations for Their Future

Responsibility fell heavy on Nanette as she delved deeper and deeper into all the details of making the transition for Pete from his life he currently had to one with her. There were so many details to work out – where to begin. Nanette assured Pete that by taking one issue at a time, they would get through that issue with the help of all the family, doctors, and professionals they had working with them. This would happen but it would take time.

Soon after the holidays, Pete and Nanette met with a team of folks from all aspects of Pete's life.

Dr. Harkins spoke first. "You know Pete, this is a great move you are about to encounter. This is going to take a great effort on your part to make such a huge adjustment to life. Your emotional and mental state will depend on how much you truly want this vast change in your life."

"I am well aware that there will be some big changes, Dr. Harkins," replied Pete. I haven't done this on a whim. Nanette and I have discussed a lot of things and we have spent a lot of time together. I have had a chance to meet most of her neighbors several times, so making a move to her house I think will be okay."

"It goes far beyond just moving into Nanette's house, Pete," interjected Stan. You have to think about losing your support system and your housing subsidy. Your Social Security might change and you will lose you medical insurance."

"I won't lose my housing subsidy," responded Pete. "Or my social security."

"Yes, honey, you will lose your housing subsidy," responded Nanette. "However, Stan, once Pete and I are married, I can add him on to my medical insurance. That should not be an issue. I don't know about the Social Security Disability benefits but we'll have to look into that. That is Federal and it should be fine no matter where he goes."

"Since you will be moving to a new town, you won't be eligible for the assistance and support of AILA, Pete," commented Julie Laughlin. "All the years, 14 to be exact, of weekly visits will stop."

"I'm okay," replied Pete now getting very jittery. They were all coming up with one reason after another why getting married to Nanette was a bad thing.

"As long as you are still living in the state, Pete, you will continue to get the assistance of DMR," spoke Judy Collins from the agency. "That will stay intact for you."

"If Pete moves in with me, there is no reason for him to worry about a housing subsidy," said Nanette. "It is my house. I have been paying the mortgage and the bills right along. Oh, yeah I am sure my bills will go up a bit with an added person, but I'm sure we can handle that. Pete is still working and I'm sure he will continue to receive something on his Social Security. That will help with some of the increase in bills. So the idea of losing his housing shouldn't be a consideration to be horribly concerned with. I am more concerned about how Pete will handle moving, and integrating himself into a new neighborhood and living with a woman on a full-time basis – one he cannot just move away from when times may get rough – and they probably will. There are always rough patches in any relationship."

"Well I think it is a large consideration for Pete to lose his housing subsidy," Stan replied in a sour response. "As you said, Pete may get tired of the new environment and want to return to his old life. That won't be so easy to do. Once he loses his subsidy for housing, it will be all but impossible to get it returned. I think it is a large consideration. What if Pete decides suddenly one day that he doesn't want to get married and live in your house? What then? The family will be left with the pieces to pick up."

"I'm not going to change my mind, Stan," returning in an irritated response. "I love Nanette and we're going to spend the rest of our lives together."

Stan and Ellie looked hard at each other. They had lived with Pete for all his life and had seen his pattern of behavior since his injury some 28 years ago. Pete never stuck with anything for a very long period of time and they were very concerned this was another passing fancy. What would they do if Pete decided this was not the course of events he wanted to have happen to him? Yet, they both wanted Pete to be happy and it was very apparent that Nanette was filling a large void that Pete was feeling in his life. They felt very trapped in this situation and were very concerned about how to handle the course of events that were unraveling. They had finally gotten Pete in a safe environment and were peaceful feeling he was being properly cared for from a lot of folks. Ellie was looking in on him or having him for dinner once or twice a week – Pete had become her weekend entertainment until Nanette came into the picture. She had to find other things to do which was not a problem, but she didn't want to invade their lives by being a hovering mother-in-law now. Ellie and Stan felt a little overwhelmed at all the prospects of future problems.

"We might be able to solve one issue," replied Julie. "Pete, what would you think of driving over to see me on a weekly basis? It's not that far for you to drive, and we could have lunch together, or play cribbage and catch up on anything that might be troubling you. How does that sound?"

"That would be fine," replied Pete. "I can do that, no problem."

"I think that would take care of some social issues and perhaps Pete for the first while after your move, it might be beneficial if we saw each other once a week also," said Dr. Harkins. "Do you think you could also manage that for a few weeks at least?"

"Sure, I can do that, too," responded Pete.

"Well, I think we are solving some issue," interjected Ellie Gallagher for the first time. "Now what will you do with all your furniture and personal possessions? Will you continue to keep up with your support groups? I think that will be important."

"He will move whatever he needs to into my house," responded Nanette. "I have a house that is not full by any means at this point, although moving in Pete's things will fill it up fast, I'm sure."

"I'll look into the Social Security issue," replied Stan a bit more unnerved by the course of events. "It seems like you continue to have a support team and have added a new person to your list, Pete – Nanette!"

"I sure have, Stan," replied Pete. "She's a gem and the love of my life. She's everything I could ask for."

"We're a team," commented Nanette.

"Seems like we have accomplished a lot today and perhaps we can meet next month to see how everyone has achieved the various aspects of going through all these changes for Pete," said Dr. Harkins. "In the meantime, you two, I want to make sure you both continue to see Dr. Cutler every week. I think that was a very important thing you did on your own and it appears to be having a great influence on both of you."

"We will, Dr. Harkins," responded Nanette. "I feel it is important too because that is the only way we both focus on all the baggage we *both* bring to this relationship."

The meeting ended with everyone having a small bit of details to work on to try to make all the pieces fit together. There was a lot to consider and a lot of work that lay ahead for Nanette and Pete. That evening while Nanette was making dinner, she noticed Pete sitting at the dining room table with his head bent in a very sad manner. When she turned to speak to him, he wasn't there. Oh, he was there physically, but his mind had wandered off somewhere. Pete II had come to reside for a short while.

"Pete, I don't like this other Pete being here," said Nanette in a very high-pitched sharp voice. "Go away."

The moment Nanette spoke, Pete looked up at Nanette with a huge smile and said, "I'm here, honey. He's gone. Thanks."

That was the very last time ever for Pete II to show himself again. Nanette had succeeded in permanently getting this other personality of Pete's to never show himself again. To her credit, Nanette was learning very diligently how to handle the various sides of Pete.

"I am a bit nervous about all the things that we have to do just so we can get married and live our lives together," responded Pete.

"Don't worry, sweetie," said Nanette. "Everyone has to make sacrifices when they decided to marry. Marriage is built on compromises and we are no different. Let's just take one issue and one day at a time. Give it time, Pete. Patience is a good word for you to learn and practice. It will take a lot of patience for both of us."

The days moved forward and the progress seemed to move more slowly for Pete and Nanette than either of them would have liked. They continue to visit Dr. Cutler every week, which offered them great insights on the meaning of patience. Those visits were some of the hardest and yet the most influential discussions that happened between the two of them. The ideas and thoughts that Dr. Cutler offered gave way to many meaningful solutions to some of the issues that lay before this couple so in love and desiring to make life correct.

One month later the same group met again under the guidance of Dr. Harkins and Julie Laughlin. This time there was a bit more optimism within the group.

Dr. Harkins opened the meeting saying, "Welcome everyone. I do believe we each have a lot to report to one another and that Pete and

Nanette have moved considerably along in their preparations. I for one am more confident that Nanette is prepared and confident to handle the ramifications of sharing her life with Pete with all his shortfalls – not to undermine any of your strengths Pete."

"I did find out from Social Security that Pete's benefits should remain in place even after their marriage," replied Stan. "That is a plus for them, however, I am still a bit concerned about Pete giving up his apartment. Is there any way he could keep his apartment and still move temporarily in with Nanette?"

"No Stan, that is not a possibility," responded Julie. "We have a lot of residents who are anxious to have that apartment and we could not just hold it on the possibility that Pete might return. That is not an option."

"What are you thinking, Stan," replied Pete. "When I move in with Nanette, I intend to stay with her forever. Besides I am there already more than I am at the apartment – I have a new home already." No one in this room knew that Pete and Nanette had already committed themselves to one another in the eyes of God in their own private ceremony. As far as the two of them were concerned they were already married and together for life.

"Well, Pete, when do you and Nanette think you want to move your things?" commented Ellie.

"Right away," said Pete.

"The lease is up on the apartment at the end of March," said Julie. "Perhaps it would be good to plan on having the apartment empty by the end of March; that way I can rent it out quickly to another resident without a problem with the landlord."

"That's more than six weeks away!" exclaimed Pete.

"That's fine, honey," said Nanette. "It will give us time to get the house ready for your things and plan where we intend to put some of your furniture. That will be fine. It will give us time to pack up your things and prepare for the move."

"I'll get a truck and we'll plan to move your heavy stuff out the last weekend in March," said Stan. "Perhaps one of your sons could help me move him, Nanette?"

"Sure, I'll ask them. I think that Jake will be more available than the others. Can't really ask Teddy since he has a bad back, and Jamie is in Washington, but I'm sure Jake can help."

"Sounds like things are moving along the way you wanted, Pete," said Dr. Harkins.

"Yes, they are, but I wish it was happening faster," said Pete.

"You are so impatient, Pete," said Nanette. You are going to have some tough lessons in patience over the next several months. It will all happen but as I have told you before, let's just take one issue at a time, one day at a time."

"I like the way this woman thinks," said Ellie. "You seem to have Pete's best interest at heart, Nanette and for that I am very grateful. He needs a lot of understanding and patience. I think you two will be fine, just plan things out before you jump into anything. Life is simpler that way."

The following weeks took on a life of their own. Moving Pete from his apartment to the house was a full time job and there still was a wedding to plan. Nanette and Pete packed boxes after boxes and with Ellie's help, made decisions as to what they would take for personal possession and what they might donate. A few items found themselves in the trash either because they were too worn out or too broken to try a new home. The moving day was fast approaching and they still needed to secure the church and find a place for their reception for their approaching wedding.

The week before Pete moved into Nanette's new home, they met with Pastor Jason Schneider from their Community Church. Although there was some resistance on the part of Pastor Schneider about the possibility of a solid marriage between them, he continued with the pre-marriage counseling and gave them both materials to be read, completed and returned to him. He locked in the date at the church and made plans to meet them again to discuss their written materials.

"Moving day is here," said Pete. "Let get up and get going. Jake and Stan will be at the apartment at 8:00 a.m. and I want to be there before them. Move it lady!"

"I'm coming, I'm coming," replied Nanette rubbing her sleepy eyes. There was always more work ahead and today would be a particularly tiring day.

Jake and Stan arrived at the apartment about half an hour after Pete and Nanette. The truck was loaded by these two able-bodied men and off to Nanette's home within two hours. Pete and Nanette met the truck at her house and as things moved in her new home, she wondered where on earth there would be room for her and Pete to move. Everything became cluttered in a matter of minutes. She took in a deep breath and knew that the next few weeks would be very busy trying to find places to put Pete's furniture and possessions. She knew she could store some of his things until they had more time to figure out what and where things should be stored. The evening couldn't arrive soon enough and Pete and Nanette crashed hard on the sofa as all the extra people left. Now miscellaneous cartons and odd pieces of furniture surrounded them, which they would deal with tomorrow. At least all of Pete's clothes found places in a closet or drawers in a bureau. That was one problem they didn't have to face later on. Thanks to Ellie, she had convinced Pete to discard a lot of old clothes that either were worn out or had holes in them – a difficult task to get Pete to part with any piece of clothing.

The following morning Nanette was up early again to try to decipher where to store some of these cartons and miscellaneous items. The family room in the basement seems a likely place for many items at least for now. Pete and Nanette would have weeks and months to take care of these few items. They also needed to return to the apartment and clean-up for the next tenants.

"We have to begin checking out places for receptions, Pete," said Nanette. "It may be difficult to get our date as we only have a little more than a year before the wedding and places book early."

"Where do you think we should look?" asked Pete.

"Let me begin by making some phone calls and asking for the date. Then we can make a more logical decision based on what I find out."

Over the next several days, Nanette made more than 50 phone calls to various restaurants and caterers to get turned down for the date by most of them. There were three that had the date available but the prices seemed way out of reach for their budget. Nanette knew they needed to keep the cost down in order to have a nice wedding without going overboard. There were other things that were important to each of them and the service was to be their main focus. The 'party' afterwards would be lovely but they wanted the service to be meaningful for them.

"We have appointment within the next couple of weeks to visit each of the three restaurants I think might be okay for us," said Nanette. "One is tomorrow evening. Will that be okay for you, Pete?"

"That's fine but have you thought about having a caterer in a hall or perhaps we can have it at my mother's Country Club?" responded Pete.

"I hardly think we can afford your mother's Country Club, but we can look into it," replied Nanette. "The first thing we need to do is plan on a guest list and get it into some type of manageable size."

"We have to invite the entire church, since that is where we met," said Pete.

"Pete, we can't afford to do that!" exclaimed Nanette. "Our families together will be over 100 people and with all the church there wouldn't be even enough seats in the church to seat everyone for the ceremony. I don't want some of our families to not have a seat for the service. Then if that isn't enough of a consideration, there isn't a place large enough to hold 500 people or funds in our budget to afford such an elaborate reception."

"We have a problem," said Pete.

"No, we just have to think about it," replied Nanette.

So they sat together that evening and pondered over a guest list for hours. They made a decision to include only those folks from church whom they had served on a committee or group of some kind with – since they were both active that still made a large list. Then Nanette came to her senses.

"Pete, we can't do all this!" explained Nanette in a very worried voice. "There is no way your brain will handle all these people around you at once. This is never going to work."

"We have to make it work, Nanette," said Pete. "I want all these people at our wedding. There has to be a way to work this all out."

Nanette thought the details of moving Pete in to the house were bad enough, now there were the considerations that Pete might have a breakdown if he was subjected to hundreds of people at him at one time. How would she make this happen for Pete the way he had dreamed of his entire life? He wanted this wedding and all these details were important to work on so that the wedding would not create problems for Pete that neither of them were prepared to handle.

"We will have to get married early in the morning," said Pete. "That is when I am my best. The earlier we plan our wedding the better."

"Okay," said Nanette. "How about 10:30 a.m. – do you think that would be good?"

"Oh no," said Pete. "We will have to make it about 8:30 a.m."

"There is no way we are going to get married at 8:30 a.m., Pete Gallagher," replied Nanette emphatically. "Perhaps 9:30 a.m., but not 8:30 a.m. Do you have any idea what a bride has to go through to prepare for her wedding?"

"No, of course, not," said Pete. "I've never done this before, remember! But I'm learning real fast. Okay, 9:30 a.m. then.

That evening the pair met with one restaurateur and realized they could have a brunch at about 12:00 or 1:00 p.m. His restaurant could accommodate about 150 people more or less. His menu was extensive and seemed perfect for the couple. He was able to put the wedding party upstairs and had a room for the happy couple to change after the reception. The only small problem would be that Pete and Nanette would have to come in from the main dining room, but since everything else seemed perfect, this was a minor detail they could overcome. Pete was not comfortable making an entrance to his wedding reception having to walk down a flight of stairs. They still had to meet two other restaurateurs before making their decision, but in the end they were sure this would accommodate what they had in mind, if they could

Cut the wedding list by about two thirds. A problem that Nanette thought she would have a lot of difficulty convincing Pete to do.

The days were filled with so many details to work out but Nanette worked very hard at trying to resolve each issue as they thought about them. She had to use every creative gene in her body to resolve issues that would normally been a non-issue in other circumstances. Nanette's days were filled to over brimming with working a full time job, commuting in heavy traffic, preparing dinner for her and Pete, and then getting him to focus on some issue related to preparing for their wedding. She had no idea that planning a wedding could be so tedious and time-consuming.

Two days later Pete and Nanette met with the Manager of the Country Club to talk about having their reception there. That was a very short visit as the couple learned in short order the price of such a reception and the fact that they could only hold between 60 to 80 people which they both knew they would never be able to cut their guest list to such a small number having such large families on both sides.

"Pete, we really have to think about cutting the guest list way down," said Nanette after dinner the following evening.

"I know, but I have a hard time not inviting folks from the church," replied Pete. "It just doesn't seem fair since so many people have known each of us for so long and watched while our romance 'budded' into the love we have for each other. So many people from the church want to see us get married."

"That's it!" exclaimed Nanette.

"What is?"

"They want to see us get married!"

"Yeah, so what large bombshell just went off in your head, please tell?"

"We'll invite them to just the wedding," said Nanette.

"We can't do that!" squealed Pete. "That would be rude."

"Well, I don't have any other great ideas at the moment," replied Nanette. "Do you?"

"No, I can't say that I do!" responded Pete.

That weekend they were invited to Connie's parents for dinner on Saturday night and to play a game or two with Teddy, Connie, and her mother, Mary Daley. They arrived a few minutes before 5:00 p.m. with a salad in hand to share with everyone. Dinner was delightful and they were enjoying everyone's company. Teddy and Connie cleared the table and pulled out a board game, Tabo. The foursome began playing and laughing so hard that their sides were beginning to explode. In the middle of the second round, Nanette's cell phone rang.

"Hello," said Nanette.

"Oh hi, how are you," said Penny Murphy, Nanette's long-time friend from her childhood.

"We're great," explained Nanette. "We're over to Connie's parents playing Tabo with Teddy, Connie and Mary and laughing until we hurt. How are things with you?"

"They're great, but I won't keep you long if you're visiting and having a good time," responded Penny. "I just wanted to share some news with you. I am giving you a week of one of my timeshares as your wedding present in Hawaii. Do you think Pete would like that?"

"What? Are you kidding?" screamed Nanette. "Yeah, he would like that and so would I. You can't do that! Oh, wow!" Nanette was beside herself. She hadn't given much thought to their honeymoon. With spending money daily on wedding plans, she wasn't sure there would be much of a honeymoon. She sure wanted to go somewhere wonderful particularly because they would both need to be far away and relax after so many activities in their lives.

"Yeah, I'm serious," replied Penny. "It's all set. You two will have a week on me in Maui. Happy wedding, you two!"

"How can I ever thank you enough?" responded Nanette.

"No need – you just did," said Penny. "Enjoy yourselves tonight and on your honeymoon. Need to run, take care!"

"Thanks, and have a great weekend," returned Nanette. She hung up her phone and starred at Pete for several moments before being able to speak.

"What is it honey?" said Pete. "You look like a bombshell just landed. What's up?"

"We're going to Hawaii for our honeymoon!" exclaimed Nanette.

"Are you serious?" questioned Pete.

"Yeah, Penny is giving us a week of her timeshare there!" explained Nanette.

"Wow, Mom!" said Teddy. "That is some gift. You two are very lucky to have Penny for a friend. She is so kind and always doing something special for someone and that someone is often you, Mom!"

"I know, Teddy," said Nanette. "I have very often been the recipient of many of her lovely ideas and gifts. We are very fortunate, once again! What a special friend."

Pete was so excited he had a very hard time focusing on playing the game anymore. He couldn't explain his immense feeling of gratitude to Penny for making a trip like this possible. This was more than he ever thought possible! Living on the east coast made thinking about a trip to Hawaii near impossible much less to be able to share such a trip with Nanette. This would be something very special indeed!

The days continued to be full of plans and preparations but it was difficult to move very far forward with a looming invitation list of more than 400 people. Nanette was nervous she would never be able to get Pete to reduce the number of people and she knew they could not afford a reception for that many people much less even find a restaurant that would hold that many people.

Two weeks later they attended their church as usual and enjoyed the sermon that Pastor Schneider delivered. He reminded them that they needed to complete their paperwork and hand it in to him. He then wanted to see them again once he had a chance to study their comments. After the service, Pete and Nanette joined other members in the fellowship hall for refreshments. A young woman who used to watch Teddy when he was small, greeted Nanette. Ruby Watkins was an active member of church and had attended all her life. She knew all the ins and outs of the church and was an assiduous worker in many areas of church life.

"Hey, Nanette," said Ruby. "How are things going?"

"They're good," replied Nanette. "Lots to do to plan this wedding for us and particularly to think about all the details to make it as smooth for Pete as possible."

"If you need any help, I'd be more than happy to do so!" explained Ruby. "You know I am a Wedding Consultant and have done many of these in the past."

"No, I didn't know that," said Nanette, "but I'll keep that in mind." Nanette moved on to talk to other folks without thinking much about what she just had heard.

The days continued to move on and still they hadn't settled on a place for their reception and time was getting shorter each day. Now they might run into the possibility that the date wouldn't be free at local restaurants. It was the middle of the week when Nanette suddenly came up with a wonderful solution.

"Pete, I have the best idea yet!" Nanette said in excitement overwhelming to Pete.

"What is it?" he said.

"Why don't we have a stand-up reception at church?" replied Nanette. "Ruby Watkins offered to help me with wedding plans and perhaps she would have some suggestions on how we could do that. That way our worries would be over."

"You mean have our wedding reception at the church?" questioned Pete.

"Yeah, in the fellowship hall!"

"No, no, no!" Pete replied emphatically.

"Why not?" said Nanette. "It solves so many issues."

"Because I want a reception at a restaurant and I want to have a 'first dance' with my bride. I want a full party, that's why," explained Pete now getting very despondent.

"Take it easy, honey," said Nanette. "We'll work this out. There has to be a solution to this."

"Well I thought we were only inviting the people from the church that we served on a committee with or we had some connection?" questioned Pete now getting more disturbed than ever.

"We are," replied Nanette. "However, even that number will be 250 to 300 people and adding our families we will have another 150. We have to think about eliminating somehow."

"We can't eliminate," cried Pete. "I want them all." Pete was growing more and more frustrated as their conversation continued. Then as though a magic bullet sprung into Nanette's head or maybe it was another great moment from God above, Nanette had the solution.

"I've got it, Pete," exclaimed Nanette. "No more need to fret. We will invite everyone to the wedding. I'll ask Ruby to host a stand-up reception for everyone who comes to the church in the fellowship hall. We'll then invite those folks we want to include in a 'brunch' at the first restaurant we talked to – you know Allure Manor. The one that fit the budget and still would provide everything we wanted. They can seat 150 people and I think we can eliminate and mange to keep that part of the 'party' limited to fewer than 150 people. What do think about that idea?"

"I think you've done it," Pete sighed with a huge sense of relief. His idea of including everyone who meant something to him was finally coming together. This would be the most important day of his life.

The following Sunday Nanette spoke to Ruby who was more than willing to provide the services she needed. She gave Nanette a quote of $100 and she would make a wonderful reception for her at the church. Nanette explained her concern about Pete seeing so many people coming at him from the church and greeting him in the hallway that he would come apart mentally. Ruby suggested that the loving couple immediately go into the Women's Parlor further down the hallway. She would put ropes up to guide people along, and if there were spare family that could stand perched in specified areas along the rope, that would encourage folks to greet the wedding party in the parlor and then exit the opposite door. They would be directed back along the ropes and into the hall for refreshments. This would provide Pete with a break in people and he would only be subjected to a few at a time. When he was ready to greet everyone at once, he would be more prepared because he would be doing the greeting.

Plans were coming together and the following week they put a deposit on the restaurant and secured their 'brunch' for their wedding reception. Would the day that Pete looked forward to all his life actually run as smoothly as Nanette hoped? She was confident that by making it early enough in the day, Pete would be very fresh and chances for his endurance to remain for most of the day was higher. The entire wedding would be over by 4:00 p.m. and that would be good for Pete. Nanette continue to plan an escape for Pete should the need arise in a motor home outside the restaurant should he need to take a break or to rest for a time parting from so many people at one time.

There were the normal details to think about concerning Nanette's desires also. She was married in a wedding ceremony twice before and a third time was overpowering her mental capacity. What would her friends and family think – a third wedding – how ridiculous was this? She could wear a wedding gown again! Or could she?

While shopping in a mall one Saturday afternoon, they came upon a few manikins wearing wedding dresses.

"You're never going to see me in one of those!" exclaimed Nanette.

"What do you mean?" exclaimed Pete. "Are you going to deprive me of seeing my bride come down the aisle in a wedding gown?"

"It just wouldn't be appropriate, Pete," said Nanette.

Pete hung his head in despair. This was another part of his dream – his dream for his wedding and seeing his very own bride walk down the isle of their church on the day of their wedding. A time when they would commit their lives together standing in a church full of family and friends in their wedding attire. He had to change her mind.

That evening Pete brought the subject up again. "Please won't you change your mind and wear a wedding dress?"

"Pete, you just said something that I hadn't considered before," said Nanette.

"Whatever did I say that was so unusual?" questioned Pete. "I just asked a simple question."

"Yeah, you did," said Nanette. "What if I had a 'dress' made that looked like a wedding gown but wasn't white?"

"That would be okay, but what color would it be?" asked Pete.

"I want to be married in robin egg blue," she said.

"It must be long and have a train on it," he replied.

"Okay, a detachable one so I can take it off at the reception."

"That's fine, but you have to wear a veil so I can put it over your head before I kiss you."

"I'll have to think about that!" exclaimed Nanette.

This too all came together. Connie knew a friend of her mother's who made wedding dresses. She called her and the two of them came up with a wonderful idea. Nanette picked out a soft but bright robin egg blue material, white wedding organza overlay to make the material look like a wedding dress, and a wide brimmed hat with a veil that made her look like she had just stepped out of the 'Great Gatsby era'. It would be perfect and Pete was sure to approve although she would not know until he saw her that day – she would be the perfect bride for him. Nanette needed to make sure Pete would not see her dress or her the day of the wedding until she walked down the aisle, making his dream as fulfilling as possible.

Pete and Nanette continued to attend their monthly support groups for brain-injured survivors and their caregivers. The group orchestrated by Dr. Rigley, who also did a great deal of work with the Brain Injury Association in providing awareness to the public and other caregivers, was awarded a grant to develop an education video to accomplish some of Dr. Rigley's endeavors. It had been decided that Pete's story would be a real positive twist on the entire production.

One Saturday afternoon Linda Ariens came to Pete and Nanette's home for filming interviews and audio portions for the upcoming video production. Pete's story would be a voice-over at the very beginning of the video. Pete had survived his injury and moved on in a positive manner for over 30 years – how perfect to get the message out to the public that a person could achieve so much after a brain injury.

"Nanette, I have a question for you," said Linda.

"Sure, what is it, Linda?" responded Nanette.

"I'd like to film your wedding for the conclusion part of our video. Do you think that would be okay?"

"Sure, why not," giggled Nanette. "We haven't hired a photographer but instead will have a videographer. I'm sure we will have lots of folks taking still picture and cameras will be going off everywhere – what's one more! I think that will be the best part of the Group's video!"

"Great," said Linda. "I was really hoping you would approve."

Two weeks later Linda called the house to let Nanette and Pete know that not only would she be filming their wedding but that the large local city newspaper would be there taking still shots of her doing so. It would provide much needed press for the Brain Injury Association. The paper had agreed to do a great write-up about the video, which would be such a wonderful idea to help promote it into the right circles of professionals.

This wedding wasn't going to be a traditional wedding by a long shot but would be opening the doors to a lot of brain injured folks who have lost hope about living a fulfilling and productive life. It was amazing the good things that would be coming out of all their connections and community involvement – God was good – he was providing yet another means to show his love through Nanette and Pete.

The big day was fast approaching. Pete and Nanette had spent months planning every detail to make their service meaningful to them in every way and their wedding day to be a memorable occasion that hopefully Pete would always remember at least parts of it. Nanette knew that having a video was the best decision she had made because this very important day in their lives and one of Pete's lifetime dreams would be kept for all eternity and provide him a constant reminder of this moment in their lives.

"Pete I want to make sure you get plenty of rest before our wedding on Saturday," said Nanette.

"I know, honey, I will," replied Pete. If I don't have enough rest, the whole day could be ruined and who knows how my brain might react.

"We'll eat dinner early and I'll make sure you get to bed early," responded Nanette. "Wednesday, we'll order in a pizza as Shirley Celeb, our Matron of Honor, will be coming over to help us tie the ribbons on the carnations. You know, honey, the ribbons that have our names and wedding date on them, and the flowers that all the ushers will pass out to everyone in attendance during the wedding ceremony. I don't want you to get overtired helping us that night either as Thursday is our Wedding

Rehearsal and big party afterwards. Friday you should be able to get plenty of rest before getting up early on Saturday morning. With a 9:30 a.m. service, we are all going to have to get up very early. Do you think you will be okay with all this?"

"I'll be fine, dear," replied Pete. "You have been so considerate in all the planning and preparation to make sure I would get plenty of rest in between all the activities leading up to our wedding. Besides I'll have Friday night free and will be staying in a hotel room with Stan that night. I'm sure we'll have a simple evening.

Nanette and Pete had spent every spare minute planning and preparing every tiny detail of the wedding trying to accommodate Pete's desire for a traditional wedding and Nanette's concerns that Pete wouldn't have a mental breakdown due to all the commotion caused by all the parties and activities surrounding the wedding. She desperately wanted to marry Pete, but at the same time knew that a surge of so many things could trigger some adverse reaction in Pete's mind.

Nanette had even planned to delay the departure for their honeymoon to Hawaii by one day in order to ensure Pete was rested for the next leg in excitement over the marriage. It was a positive move on her part as she had totally forgotten that the day after their wedding was Mother's Day. This made a perfect plan for Jake, Jamie, and Teddy to pull together a family brunch right at the airport hotel to celebrate Mother's Day with their mother and Grandmother Peters.

Shirley had come and helped Nanette and Pete tie the carnations on Wednesday evening. The wedding rehearsal and dinner on Thursday following had been so special. The wedding party consisted of Shirley Celeb and Jane Gallagher who would be bridesmaids for Nanette, and Stan and Billy who would be Ushers or Groom's men for Pete. Nanette's three sons would walk her down the aisle; Teddy and Jamie first, and then Jake would escort his mother. The entire wedding party, dates and families attended the rehearsal dinner held at the Masonic Temple where Nanette had been an active member of the Order of Eastern Star for many years – it was a perfect place for their party. Nanette's Star Chapter provided a delightful buffet and because of her Star friends, Nanette found a ventriloquist friend to entertain the group. It was a perfect way to get the tension to leave Pete and Nanette witnessed him letting go and relaxing. Pete was enjoying the evening and she knew this was another good decision. She was hopeful that Saturday's events would run so smoothly.

Friday evening Shirley had planned to stay overnight with Nanette. It wasn't until late in the day that Nanette realized that Pete was expected to attend yet another party at the Club with his family. She and Shirley were invited to join them but she knew that would not work well if they were to get up at 3:00 a.m. and still look rested for the wedding at 9:30 a.m. – they would need their *beauty sleep*! With all of Nanette's planning, Pete was not going to get the rest on Friday evening she had hoped for. She prayed that Saturday would not be a problem for Pete because now he had gotten overtired. She had to rely on the instincts of his family to ensure he got the rest he needed. Perhaps partying was a way for Pete to relax and not get anxious thinking about the next day.

Jake and Jamie also stayed overnight with Nanette on Friday evening. On cue, Nanette arose and showered at 3:00 a.m. followed by Shirley. The women woke the young men at 5:15 a.m. as the house would soon be filled with a hairdresser and make-up people. Jake dressed and drove to the flower shop to pick up the necessary flowers for the church and reception and Jamie drove to the local grocery store to get the last of the cut flowers, corsages, and boutonnieres. Teddy had more than his share of tasks to do as he was singing a solo and a duet and needed to arrive at the church early to practice for the first and only time with the harpist and organist. Everything was falling in place as the happy couple planned.

Everyone arrived at the church ready to see this happy couple take their vows they had waited so long to do. Although they were already married in their hearts and before God, Pete and Nanette would commit themselves to one another legally before all their families and friends. Every detail came together as they planned and the wedding march began.

Jamie and Teddy walked down the aisle as Jake escorted his mother behind them letting the two ladies in charge make sure the train of her wedding dress was perfect – the train that Pete requested, and Nanette provided in order to please her man! Pete met Nanette's eyes and saw his beautiful bride descend down the isle of their church. He was the happiest man alive – he was getting married to the most wonderful woman he ever met.

Every detail of the ceremony came through to perfection and Pete handled every situation almost perfectly. He was so anxious to kiss his bride that Pastor Schneider had to stop him because there was one more song or one more thing that had to be done. The flowers were passed out to everyone under the direction of the Pastor as he told them it was a symbol of the love that God had given to Nanette and Pete and it was their desire to pass it on. Everyone sang the hymn, "You Want to Pass it On" and Pete and Nanette lighted their unity candle and passed roses on to each of their mother.

The time had finally come, and Pete lifted the veil that he so wanted Nanette to wear away from her beautiful face and laid it gently behind her white hat with the soft blue flowers. He tilted her chin toward him and kissed his new bride with a passion only presentable in a public church. He was now legally married before all his family and friends. Pete turned holding Nanette's hand in his and as she guided him down the steps of the chancel was painfully aware of his partially paralyzed left leg and the limp that would follow as he walked his bride down the aisle on their wedding day. It was all overshadowed as everyone witnessed the happiness in the faces of the new Mr. and Mrs. Pete Gallagher, and clapped as the new couple proceeded down the aisle to begin their carefully planned out reception. Now they could officially begin their new married life, legally "and" in the eyes of God the Father.

Chapter XV

Following the Celebration and Return to Regular Life

Nanette and Pete spent two and a half weeks seeing the sights of three of Hawaii's beautiful islands. Between helicopter ridges, viewing volcanoes, and bathing in the sunshine, Pete and Nanette had time to bask in the love of each other leaving worldly influences behind for the time being.

Upon their return to the states, they were able to visit Pete's brother, Billy and his family in California and continue their sightseeing adventures – a first for Nanette having never traveled further west than the Mississippi River.

Now they needed to focus on life as a married couple and all the challenges of marriage. The added baggage that both brought into the marriage would raise its ugly head from time to time, but thanks to their faith, both Pete and Nanette learned that patience was a mighty virtue which gave each the ability to cope with the hills and valleys of married life.

Pete and Nanette settled into her house in Connecticut and after a very short period of time, Pete was able to gain much better employment at a law firm and three years later at an architectural firm having constant interpersonal relationships with other employees of the firms. Pete learned how to manage his day-to-day life and anticipate his ups and downs as part of life. He came home to Nanette every night knowing that his job was only part of his life and the most important part was waiting for him at home.

Neither Pete nor Nanette had any real idea of what lie ahead for them as a married couple. They certainly planned and prepared for months, but all of life's challenges and rewards can never be fully realized until each person is faced with any particular situation. The choices we each make in how we react to those situations really depends on so many variables in our individual lives. Pete and Nanette would face situations very differently and those differences would bring about confusion, frustration, and irritability for both of them.

The way they chose to deal with their frustrations was very different than most couples – it is call effective communication. Pete's years of psychiatric care prepared him well to understand the need to talk about feelings before they festered into some serious and out-of-control issues.

For Nanette with her years of baggage, these were tough lessons to learn, but Pete was a patient teacher. Nanette's second marriage of physical, mental, and emotional abuse instilled bad habits in her. She grew up in a peaceful environment with her parents never seeming to have any arguments or disagreements. She was constantly confused as to why there should be any confrontations of any kind.

Pete would never settle for a dictatorship, much like Nanette saw between her parents. This newly married couple had to grow and learn from one another how to respond to each other's feelings. Nanette required a lot of emotional care and Pete had some problems realizing the difference between giving her the emotional support she needed versus sexual encounters. As much as that was special and enjoyable for both of them, Nanette required difference responses. The new couple continued to work with Dr. Cutler to sort through many of these issues. However, in spite of these roadblocks, Nanette and Pete were so happy together and shared so many wonderful times. These issues were minor and they each received a large daily dose of tremendous love from their spouses, and frequently leaned on the Lord to direct them through prayer together and individually.

With two of Nanette's sons, now their sons, embarking on large weddings, yet another challenged faced them both. It was a stressful time to prepare for a child getting married, and for Pete who had so recently become a "step-father" to three grown sons, he was a bit confused as to what his role was supposed to be.

Nanette called Jamie to verify the wedding rehearsal dinner.

"I would love to have the dinner at our home," said Nanette.

"No, Mom, you shouldn't go through all that," answered Jamie.

"Oh it's no problem," replied Nanette. "I'd be pleased to do so."

"No, Mom, it's not necessary."

"But I want to do it for you."

"No, Mom, really you don't have to. Candice's Mom can have it at her house."

"But I'm supposed to do this for you, Jamie," replied Nanette now hurt to the core.

"No, no, it's okay," said Jamie. "Got to go now. I'll talk to you later about this." Jamie hung up without the problem being resolved.

Nanette felt so inadequate. She had limited funds, with her own wedding draining them and also knowing there would be another one within a few short months she would need to do the same for. Nanette didn't think Pete could handle hearing her concerns and frustration, but also knew their pack to talk things out.

"Pete, Jamie doesn't want me to arrange the rehearsal dinner," said Nanette.

"Why not?" exclaimed Pete. "Isn't that the job as mother-of-the-groom?"

"Yeah, it is by the etiquette books," replied Nanette. "He said that his future mother-in-law could have it at her house."

"That's not right," said Pete. "That's just not right. I'm going to call him and give him a piece of my mind. What's his number? Give me his number. I'm going to let him know just who is boss here. He's not going to do this to you."

"Calm down, Pete," shouted Nanette. "This is exactly why I wasn't going to tell you any of this. I knew you'd get more upset than I would and I don't want you to talk to him at all.

"Well, someone should and why not me?" exclaimed Pete. "I ought to be able to resolve this issue once and for all."

"I'll call him tomorrow evening when we both can talk about it further," said Nanette. "In the meantime, I want you to settle down. I have everything under control. Jamie and I will work this out.

Scenes like this happened often for Pete and as much as he wanted the role of "father" and be the almighty forceful influence in the family, doing so really upset him more than it should. Nanette would feel so bad telling him things that she knew he would get upset over and eventually she learned just when to tell him the things he should know about but usually after a solution had been put in place. This way Nanette kept her promise of telling him everything, but also had the issues resolved before Pete had a chance to get upset over anything.

Nanette did resolve the issue of the rehearsal dinner and she and Jamie agreed upon a restaurant with Jamie picking up the liquor tab in order to help the finances. It worked out fine after a few conversations and this particular issue that had been a mountain for Pete, Nanette was able to see it through to a simple conclusion.

Over the next several months, Nanette and Pete dealt with various aspects of both Jamie's wedding happening in October and Teddy's wedding in January. They worked hard helping Teddy and Connie prepare table centerpieces, invitations, favors and the like for their wedding. Connie's mother was overwhelmed with the amount of things to do for a formal wedding. Candice's wedding was not as detailed for Nanette and Pete. She had a mother who took everything in stride and a sister who was more than willing to help with everything. Candice also had a lot of girlfriends eager to be on the scene and help tremendously with the preparation work. As a result, Candice did not have to worry about the details of her wedding being handled correctly. That gave Nanette and Pete a breather and more time to focus helping Teddy and Connie.

Among the preparation of the two weddings, their own Matron-of-Honor, Melanie was embarking on a horrible divorce after just getting settled into a new home they built. It was a difficult time for Melanie and without her family living in Connecticut, she turned to Nanette and Pete for help. Many evenings were spent having Melanie and Jarrett, her four-year old son for dinner and occasionally overnight. They spent many weekends together either planning a play time, or just visiting. Melanie needed good friends and Nanette and Pete were there for her when she needed them.

Melanie was forced to sell the new home and was fortunate enough to be able to buy a home of her own. Pete and Nanette were there to help her both physically and emotionally make the move to a new home and neighborhood for her and Jarrett. This was another situation that Pete never could have prepared himself for. For that matter, neither could Nanette. They found themselves exhausted trying to give Melanie and Jarrett the time they needed in the middle of their son's wedding preparation – a difficult combination.

Jamie and Candice were married in October in a beautiful fall church ceremony. Candice arrived at the church in a beautiful white horse-drawn carriage with her attendants in an open carriage following. What a beautiful bride for Jamie. They had a lovely reception afterwards and Nanette was so proud of Pete. He managed to get himself through the ceremony and reception just fine although he continued to watch Nanette or someone he knew all the time. He was learning very well how to be in a large crowd without having an emotional outburst. Nanette was very successful in training him to focus on her or someone in close proximity to him that he knew rather than look at the whole crowd. If Nanette was next to Pete and holding on to his arm, she could talk to him softly about the things happening around them. Pete was a quick learner and was able to absorb these crowd situations in no time.

Pete and Nanette had only a short while to settle down from Jamie and Connie's wedding until the Thanksgiving and Christmas holidays were upon them. More crowds for Pete to be subjected to, but he did seem to love visiting family and friends and was such a social person. The activities around two large families and trying to divide themselves between each family grew very tiring for both of them. Nanette was still on a learning curve as to how to hold Pete from overdoing – a good lesson for her to learn as she was also aging. She was grateful for the excuses to be able to go home to rest awhile before having to move on to the next excitement of the week.

"We are going over to Teddy and Connie's apartment after dinner tonight to help finish the table centerpieces, Pete," said Nanette. "Are you okay with that?"

"Sure, that's great," said Pete.

"You think you can help to cut and tie ribbon until your fingers hurt," said Nanette.

"Sure, whatever you need, honey," responded Pete.

He was always willing to help where he was needed. If he didn't know how to do something, he was more than willing to be instructed and attempt to learn. For the most part, Pete did extremely well. They were able to get all the decorations completed in a few sessions with five people helping at once. Teddy and Connie's wedding was approaching fast and would be another crowd situation for Pete to deal with.

It was a cold day in January in Connecticut when Teddy and Connie got married. With more than a foot of snow to climb over, there were more than the usual challenges. Pete and Nanette held a beautiful rehearsal dinner at the hotel where most of the wedding party stayed overnight.

Early the next morning, a limousine made several very orchestrated trips that Nanette help pull together to transport the females of the wedding party to get their beauty needs tended to and the male counterparts of the wedding party to the church on time. It was a beautiful church wedding as Teddy sang the song he wrote for his bride as his vows to her. Again, Pete managed the day in splendid fashion and Nanette felt he was really making such progress. He united with her and her large family including all the commotion surrounding them. Pete seemed to take most of the confusion in stride and enjoyed another son's beautiful wedding.

But the excitement never seemed to end for the newly married couple. Dr. Harkins had a strong message for Pete soon as he and Nanette became engaged.

"Pete, you must remember, Nanette is like a steam locomotive and you are the caboose," said Dr. Harkins. "You will never be able to catch up with her. So I don't want you to even try."

"But Dr. Harkins, she is the head of the train and I am attached – so I have to follow," said Pete.

"That's okay, Pete," replied Dr. Harkins with a chuckle. "You follow, but don't ever think you'll get ahead or even catch up to her."

"Okay, Dr. Hawkins," said Pete. "I get the point."

From that moment on, Nanette realized she had a full-time responsibility of running the family household for the most part. Pete would have plenty of input but the majority of the decision-making and thought process would probably have to come from her.

As they approached their second anniversary, Pete and Nanette made plans to take a trip to Florida where Pete would meet Nanette's dear Aunt Gracie, for the first time. They made plans to stay with her and this would be only the second time that Nanette took Pete on an airplane. Now married to Pete for two years and getting to know him better, Nanette was more comfortable in what Pete could and could not do in terms of managing to get himself around a strange place. They made the trip just fine and Aunt Gracie met them at the airport.

"So this is the famous Pete Gallagher," said Aunt Gracie. "I see what you mean about his height – like them tall don't you Nanette?" Aunt Gracie never pulled any bunches and meeting Pete would be no different.

"And I guess all of Nanette's family is short," returned Pete. Aunt Gracie had met her match and the banter between them continued in fun for the entire week. They both took an immediate liking to one another and Nanette couldn't have been happier. It proved to be a marvelous week and lots of fun visiting her special aunt.

"Pete, you know we have more activities coming up soon," said Nanette.

"Oh, great! What's going on?" asked Pete.

"My parents will be celebrating their 63rd Wedding Anniversary and Dad called to say he wanted to pay for the immediate family to go to a restaurant to celebrate," said Nanette.

"Something seems wrong with that picture," said Pete. "Shouldn't the family be treating them to the dinner?"

"That's the way Dad wants it and I don't think we are going to change his mind," said Nanette.

"Yeah, I know your Dad can be pretty set in his customs," said Pete.

"I will talk to Jake, Jamie, and Teddy and see if we can do the flowers and maybe some decorations for the dinner," said Nanette.

"That's sounds great to me," said Pete. "Let me know if I can help in any way. I love your parents and I would love to see their party just perfect for them."

Nanette worked hard with her brother Jimmy to get *this party* off the ground and running smoothly. Lee Peters had called the restaurant but because of his age he got so many details totally messed up. Jimmy called to straighten things out and Nanette followed up with a physical visit to the restaurant. This time Nanette got smart and only told Pete when all the plans were in place and where he needed to be and when.

It was a sunny fall day when Ann and Lee Peters arrived at the restaurant with Nanette and Pete to enjoy their celebration of 63 years as a married couple. A lifetime of memories and their family beside them to help with the festivities, they were a happy pair. Nanette's son Teddy saw to it that there were perfect flowers and even a bouquet for Ann to hold for pictures, balloons, and all the trimmings. Jake moved to California but flew back to Connecticut with his partner to be with his grandparents on their special day. Jamie and Candice drove up from New York City where they lived to join in the merriment. Lee and Ann Peters were aging very fast, but still adored each other immensely. It showed in every move on this – their very special day.

It was only a month later when Nanette got the phone call that Aunt Gracie wasn't doing so well and was placed in the hospital. With the urgent call that she wouldn't eat for anyone, Nanette and Pete were faced with another trip to Florida. Nanette successfully managed to get her Aunt Gracie back on her feet, in a convalescent home for a couple of weeks, and then when her cousin, Gordon Bates, returned from vacation, Aunt Gracie was moved to an assisted living facility near his home where his dad was living. Nanette only had her Aunt Gracie for three more years before her death and most of that time she was unaware of the people around her or who folks really were. Aunt Gracie only had one week to get to know Pete. This was another difficult transition for Pete to deal with Nanette's family and the ultimate age difference bringing about the inevitable end of life for her dear relatives.

Aunt Gracie died in June and the following January, Nanette and Jimmy were faced with the prospects of placing Nanette's parents in an assisted living facility. It had become very apparent that they both were not safe in their own home. They both were suffering from dementia and as hard a decision as it was, it was very apparent that their safety had to be considered. Ann Peters was lighting matches and dropping them in the trashcan still lit. Lee Peters was telling stories about people breaking into his home and how he was going to take out his shotgun and shoot the devils if they came in again.

Pete was in the middle of a family decision-making time and faced with difficult responsibilities that he had not had to experience before. Although Pete wasn't a blood relative of Nanette's family, both what he and Penny Peters thought was important to Nanette and Jimmy. So week after week, the foursome met to discuss the outcome of decisions and to make new choices for the following week or days. They worked together in a harmonious rhythm always placing the feelings of Ann and Lee Peters first. Within a few short months, Lee was taken to the hospital and later released to a nursing home. With careful planning, Nanette and Jimmy were able to get Ann Peters to an assisted living facility where Lee could join her and they could continue to live together, although not in their own home.

Lee and Ann Peters celebrated their 65th wedding anniversary with a large party at the facility where they now resided. Nanette using her planning skills once again, and saw to it that their celebration included a wedding cake, flowers, and balloons which Teddy had seen to arriving on time with the cake. The facility had planned an afternoon gathering and had a singer there. Thus, the entire community was there and helped the Peters to celebrate their 65th wedding anniversary.

Lee made family visits difficult over the last several months and carried a large amount of anger at the idea of having to live his last days in such a facility. He fought the family and judicial system hard and although he won his right to go home, Ann had not and Lee would not leave her. Within two weeks of his court battle and their anniversary, which Nanette was unable to attend, Lee Peters was taken back to the hospital with difficulty breathing. He returned for a short time to a convalescent hospital where Ann visited him only a couple of times. Lee was so angry at life itself, he gave Ann a bad time and she refused to visit him again. Lee Peters died the following January. Now heartbroken, Ann began to fail rapidly and within one month was placed in an Alzheimer's unit. Four months later, Ann suffered another small stroke and after a hospital stay, returned to the same convalescent hospital where Lee had been. She died in July probably due to a broken heart rather than any medical concerns. Ann simply stopped eating and gave up living.

"It's okay, honey," said Pete. "I'm here for you. I know how difficult this must be for you losing both your parents so quickly."

"I'm okay, Pete," replied Nanette. "They were old. They both lived a full life, they did a lot of great things in their lives, and they were great parents. I loved them both very much and I know it was their time to go." Nanette Gallagher shed very few tears at the loss of her parents. She was prepared for some time for their passing.

Pete had to allow Nanette time to tend to all the probate processing for both her parents, which took a great deal of time. He was there at every turn to help her where she needed help even if that was just delivering envelopes to the attorney. Pete knew Nanette took a lot on to marry him, but he had no idea how much he was faced to deal with at taking on a wife. He was learning fast how life changes in a heartbeat and what it really means to be someone else's partner. From time to time, Pete expressed his feelings in anger that would make Nanette stop short. However, having the great training from Dr. Harkins, Dr. Cutler and Pete himself, Nanette learned the real meaning of patience – a lesson neither Nanette Gallagher nor anyone can ever fully understand in any lifetime. It is a constant reminder to all of us that patience is the very best virtue that God has given all of us, and coupled with communication is a sure way to resolve most issues

It took Nanette several months working on paperwork to try to settle the estates of both her parents. During that time, Pete and Nanette made a life-changing decision.

During all the perplexity of taking care of Nanette's parents, Ellie Gallagher was making plans of her own to sell her home and move to an assisted living apartment. After many months of waiting for just the right apartment, Ellie Gallagher made a huge decision to move only those things she truly needed from her large home to these smaller living quarters. A large decision to let all the possessions of one's life be handed down to a younger generation – your own children and grandchildren and begin a new kind of life with only those things that make one contented.

Pete had to face another change in his life. Changes seemed to be coming rather quickly for Pete, and Nanette was very concerned how Pete would handle all the changes.

"You know, honey, you never really grew up in the house your Mom had in Farmington," said Nanette.

"Yeah, I know," said Pete. "It's just hard to see the big house go where we had so many wonderful holidays with the family."

"Those memories won't go away," said Nanette. "I know when we had to sell my parents' home it was hard, but the memories are in your head and your heart not in the building that is moving on to a new family."

"I guess you're right," said Pete. "But I will still miss the place."

It was another sense of loss for Pete, but the weeks and months to follow gave Pete new hope for a bright future. He and Nanette were forming their own memories and they were forming a new life together.

"You know, honey, we really need to think about taking a vacation," said Pete. "You've been working so hard at work, on your parents' estates, and trying to keep our house running, I really think you need some time off."

"Probably not a good time to think about vacation, Pete," responded Nanette.

"Yes, it is," replied Pete. This is the best time of all. You really need a break."

"Well, where do you want to go?" questioned Nanette.

"You have been talking about retirement a lot lately and moving somewhere warm. Why don't we try to vacation somewhere we might like to retire," said Pete.

"That sounds good," said Nanette. "How about Virginia, or Georgia. We know that Florida is too hot and humid for my asthma."

"Let's try Arizona," said Pete. "My uncle had a place in Tucson and for years and years my family and I would vacation there. It's a great place and very dry."

"But Pete, it so hot there," said Nanette. "I can't imagine that being good for my asthma."

"You'd be surprised," said Pete. "As hot as it gets, it is so dry that you won't even mind the heat. I really think you might like it."

Nanette was very skeptical but agreed to a trip to Arizona. They made plans to take a timeshare unit in the heat of the year in Sedona and to travel around the state to see what it might be like. Nanette was pleasantly surprised at her first visit to the state of Arizona and only her second trip west of the Mississippi River. She fell in love with the hot weather and although Pete tried to explain to her that Sedona was cooler because it was north, Nanette was convinced this was worth looking into further.

Within a few months, Pete and Nanette took another trip to Arizona. This time they visited Peoria, which neighbors Phoenix and gave Nanette a much better view of the hot weather and what the terrain looked like when it was hot. The foliage was thinner but just as beautiful as many of the pictures Nanette had seen. There was no comparison to the east coast. The west had its own beauty in the sand, the huge mountains with the various hues of browns, greens, and reds all mixed together. She began to look at the various flowering plants and although they were so different than what she had grown up knowing, Nanette realized that these special little blossoms had a particular beauty all to their own.

After much research before this last visit, Nanette and Pete visited a "manufactured home" manufacturer. They listened to all the information and before their return to Connecticut, began the process to build their new home. Nanette decided to retire from her current position at the law firm and gain new employment in Arizona. They were going to move now rather than wait for retirement to assure they were fit and healthy to make the move and have some time to enjoy their home before any health issues took over their lives. The cold weather was bothering both of them in Connecticut and the idea of spending their later years in Arizona was a refreshing one. They would begin their lives anew together in a pleasant environment they had both longed for.

Pete was faced again with another new challenge. Having to pack and unpack boxes and boxes to make a physical move. Nanette was concerned if Pete could handle such a huge change. They each focused on one item or one room at a time. They lived around boxes and boxes for months and months. Then the offer came on their house in Connecticut and the time to move was upon them. They only had a week to get the movers there and leave.

Careful planning on Nanette's part, they sent their precious doggie on first for her to stay in a kennel while they made their last minute preparations. Two days later, the movers arrived and loaded the contents of their home. They spent five days in a hotel room while they tied up loose ends including the probate process for Nanette's parents. They visited with family and friends to say good-bye. They arrived in Phoenix, AZ in April and Nanette secured a new position in a law firm the following day. They spent another week in another hotel while their belongings were to arrive to their new apartment and they could get settled in.

Again, Pete handled the move in such wonderful spirits and as best as anyone would. Nanette thought he did much better than she did with all the commotion and fussing over all the details. The couple remained in their new apartment for nine months while their new home was being built.

The serious frustration for both Nanette and Pete came when they found the perfect community to put their new manufactured home, but they couldn't make the deal happen. They negotiated back and forth for months before they finally made the biggest deal of their lives – where they would live in their new community. They would enjoy the company of other folks their own ages. They would enjoy many activities offered at the club house, and they would now be able to spend hours and hours at the lake watching the fountain and the many fish swim – along with their precious "doggie" they would continue to live the life they had both dreamed about for so many years – individually and now they would do it together – they would live the life of their parents in a harmonious love nest!

Epilogue

Pete had now achieved two of the largest dreams of his life – the dreams his family said he would never realize – he now had a wife and three stepsons who he was so proud to call his own.

Pete and Nanette's move to Phoenix, Arizona in April of 2006 was successful. After their nine-month stint of apartment living, they settled into their astonishing retirement community and began to enjoy their new friends. Her parents' estates still were unsettled but Nanette dragged all the paperwork with her and was able to complete the Probate matters in a few months. Pete retired once they moved, as gaining positive employment for a brain-injured person was not possible in Arizona. Nanette was not about to let Pete sit idly by and let him turn into a television zombie.

They found a marvelous and spirit-filled church where Pete spends many hours volunteering and doing service projects. Additionally, they both have become involved as volunteers in a service ministry of their Church at the Campus of Care facilities helping folks of all ages from independent living and beyond.

Pete has become an active participant of the Men's Club in their retirement community and has found many friends in the park who not only enjoy his company, but who rely on him to help them with various projects they are unable to do.

Nanette has found a new position in a new law firm and continues to seek a positive environment where her strengths are more valuable. Her constant faith reminds her that when God feels the time for new adventures is right, her talents will become a focus in the right places. Until then, Nanette is content to wait upon the Lord.

Less than two years after their move, they faced one last challenge and test to endure – the sudden loss of Jimmy Peters, Nanette's brother. That was a devastating loss for Nanette and she didn't handle that part of her life well at all. Jimmy meant so much to Nanette from the time she was a very little girl – he was always her hero! His passing took a part of her and changed her life, as she knew it. As in all grieving circumstances, it affects everyone around including those of your household. Pete had a struggle, too, with the loss of his brother-in-law and slowly together they are continuing to feel the peace of God settle once again in their lives. It will take them both time to overcome a large junk of life being disturbed, but they are working together toward that goal.

Nanette and Peter continue to live their lives in a contented and peaceful environment and feel the greatness of God's love in each other every day. Life has settled down and the activities of regular life are far more enjoyable. Life is so precious and our time with one another so limited. They are continuing to learn how to embrace each day with an enduring and sustaining love of God and of each other.

All the Glory goes to God for the inspiration to write this story. May those who read this story, based on true facts, but told in a fictitious manner, gain the ***Power of the Grace of God*** and the ***Hope and Love*** that surpasses all human understanding. It is only with this kind of love can the human spirit achieve the impossible and understand the true feelings of the Love of God. May God bless you all!